GACE

Paraprofessional
Part 2 of 2

SECRETS

Study Guide
Your Key to Exam Success

GACE Test Review for the
Georgia Assessments for the
Certification of Educators

Dear Future Exam Success Story:

First of all, **THANK YOU** for purchasing Mometrix study materials!

Second, congratulations! You are one of the few determined test-takers who are committed to doing whatever it takes to excel on your exam. **You have come to the right place.** We developed these study materials with one goal in mind: to deliver you the information you need in a format that's concise and easy to use.

In addition to optimizing your guide for the content of the test, we've outlined our recommended steps for breaking down the preparation process into small, attainable goals so you can make sure you stay on track.

We've also analyzed the entire test-taking process, identifying the most common pitfalls and showing how you can overcome them and be ready for any curveball the test throws you.

Standardized testing is one of the biggest obstacles on your road to success, which only increases the importance of doing well in the high-pressure, high-stakes environment of test day. Your results on this test could have a significant impact on your future, and this guide provides the information and practical advice to help you achieve your full potential on test day.

Your success is our success

We would love to hear from you! If you would like to share the story of your exam success or if you have any questions or comments in regard to our products, please contact us at **800-673-8175** or **support@mometrix.com**.

Thanks again for your business and we wish you continued success!

Sincerely,
The Mometrix Test Preparation Team

Need more help? Check out our flashcards at: http://MometrixFlashcards.com/GACE

TABLE OF CONTENTS

Mathematics (continued)

Geometry and Measurement

Lines and Planes

A **point** is a fixed location in space; has no size or dimensions; commonly represented by a dot.

A **line** is a set of points that extends infinitely in two opposite directions. It has length, but no width or depth. A line can be defined by any two distinct points that it contains. A line segment is a portion of a line that has definite endpoints. A ray is a portion of a line that extends from a single point on that line in one direction along the line. It has a definite beginning, but no ending.

A **plane** is a two-dimensional flat surface defined by three non-collinear points. A plane extends an infinite distance in all directions in those two dimensions. It contains an infinite number of points, parallel lines and segments, intersecting lines and segments, as well as parallel or intersecting rays. A plane will never contain a three-dimensional figure or skew lines. Two given planes will either be parallel or they will intersect to form a line. A plane may intersect a circular conic surface, such as a cone, to form conic sections, such as the parabola, hyperbola, circle or ellipse.

Perpendicular lines are lines that intersect at right angles. They are represented by the symbol ⊥. The shortest distance from a line to a point not on the line is a perpendicular segment from the point to the line.

Parallel lines are lines in the same plane that have no points in common and never meet. It is possible for lines to be in different planes, have no points in common, and never meet, but they are not parallel because they are in different planes.

A **bisector** is a line or line segment that divides another line segment into two equal lengths. A perpendicular bisector of a line segment is composed of points that are equidistant from the endpoints of the segment it is dividing.

Intersecting lines are lines that have exactly one point in common. Concurrent lines are multiple lines that intersect at a single point.

A **transversal** is a line that intersects at least two other lines, which may or may not be parallel to one another. A transversal that intersects parallel lines is a common occurrence in geometry.

Angles

An **angle** is formed when two lines or line segments meet at a common point. It may be a common starting point for a pair of segments or rays, or it may be the intersection of lines. Angles are represented by the symbol ∠.

The **vertex** is the point at which two segments or rays meet to form an angle. If the angle is formed by intersecting rays, lines, and/or line segments, the vertex is the point at which four angles are formed. The pairs of angles opposite one another are called vertical angles, and their measures are equal.

An *acute* angle is an angle with a degree measure less than 90°.

A *right* angle is an angle with a degree measure of exactly 90°.

An *obtuse* angle is an angle with a degree measure greater than 90° but less than 180°.

A *straight angle* is an angle with a degree measure of exactly 180°. This is also a semicircle.

A *reflex angle* is an angle with a degree measure greater than 180° but less than 360°.

A *full angle* is an angle with a degree measure of exactly 360°.

Review Video: Geometric Symbols: Angles
Visit mometrix.com/academy and enter code: 452738

Two angles whose sum is exactly 90° are said to be **complementary**. The two angles may or may not be adjacent. In a right triangle, the two acute angles are complementary.

Two angles whose sum is exactly 180° are said to be **supplementary**. The two angles may or may not be adjacent. Two intersecting lines always form two pairs of supplementary angles. Adjacent supplementary angles will always form a straight line.

Two angles that have the same vertex and share a side are said to be **adjacent**. Vertical angles are not adjacent because they share a vertex but no common side.

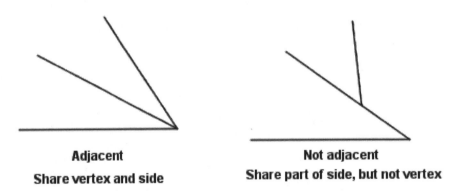

Adjacent
Share vertex and side

Not adjacent
Share part of side, but not vertex

When two parallel lines are cut by a transversal, the angles that are between the two parallel lines are **interior angles**. In the diagram below, angles 3, 4, 5, and 6 are interior angles.

When two parallel lines are cut by a transversal, the angles that are outside the parallel lines are **exterior angles**. In the diagram below, angles 1, 2, 7, and 8 are exterior angles.

When two parallel lines are cut by a transversal, the angles that are in the same position relative to the transversal and a parallel line are *corresponding angles*. The diagram below has four pairs of corresponding angles: angles 1 and 5; angles 2 and 6; angles 3 and 7; and angles 4 and 8. Corresponding angles formed by parallel lines are congruent.

When two parallel lines are cut by a transversal, the two interior angles that are on opposite sides of the transversal are called *alternate interior angles*. In the diagram below, there are two pairs of alternate interior angles: angles 3 and 6, and angles 4 and 5. Alternate interior angles formed by parallel lines are congruent.

When two parallel lines are cut by a transversal, the two exterior angles that are on opposite sides of the transversal are called *alternate exterior angles*.

In the diagram below, there are two pairs of alternate exterior angles: angles 1 and 8, and angles 2 and 7. Alternate exterior angles formed by parallel lines are congruent.

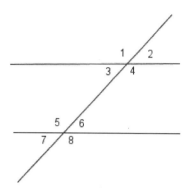

When two lines intersect, four angles are formed. The non-adjacent angles at this vertex are called vertical angles. Vertical angles are congruent. In the diagram, $\angle ABD \cong \angle CBE$ and $\angle ABC \cong \angle DBE$.

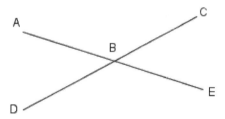

Polygons

Each straight line segment of a polygon is called a **side**.

The point at which two sides of a polygon intersect is called the **vertex**. In a polygon, the number of sides is always equal to the number of vertices.

A polygon with all sides congruent and all angles equal is called a **regular polygon**.

A line segment from the center of a polygon perpendicular to a side of the polygon is called the **apothem**. In a regular polygon, the apothem can be used to find the area of the polygon using the formula $A = \frac{1}{2}ap$, where a is the apothem and p is the perimeter.

A line segment from the center of a polygon to a vertex of the polygon is called a **radius**. The radius of a regular polygon is also the radius of a circle that can be circumscribed about the polygon.

Triangle – 3 sides

Quadrilateral – 4 sides

Pentagon – 5 sides

Hexagon – 6 sides

- 3 -

Heptagon – 7 sides

Octagon – 8 sides

Nonagon – 9 sides

Decagon – 10 sides

Dodecagon – 12 sides

More generally, an *n*-gon is a polygon that has *n* angles and *n* sides.

The sum of the interior angles of an *n*-sided polygon is $(n-2)180°$. For example, in a triangle $n = 3$, so the sum of the interior angles is $(3-2)180° = 180°$. In a quadrilateral, $n = 4$, and the sum of the angles is $(4-2)180° = 360°$. The sum of the interior angles of a polygon is equal to the sum of the interior angles of any other polygon with the same number of sides.

A **diagonal** is a line segment that joins two non-adjacent vertices of a polygon.

A **convex polygon** is a polygon whose diagonals all lie within the interior of the polygon.

A **concave polygon** is a polygon with a least one diagonal that lies outside the polygon. In the diagram below, quadrilateral *ABCD* is concave because diagonal $\overline{AC}$ lies outside the polygon.

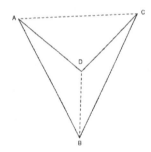

The number of diagonals a polygon has can be found by using the formula: number of diagonals = $\frac{n(n-3)}{2}$, where *n* is the number of sides in the polygon. This formula works for all polygons, not just regular polygons.

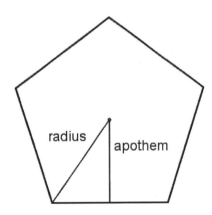

- 4 -

Congruent figures are geometric figures that have the same size and shape. All corresponding angles are equal, and all corresponding sides are equal. It is indicated by the symbol ≅.

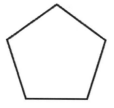 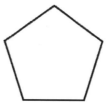

Congruent polygons

Similar figures are geometric figures that have the same shape, but do not necessarily have the same size. All corresponding angles are equal, and all corresponding sides are proportional, but they do not have to be equal. It is indicated by the symbol ~.

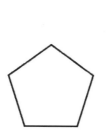 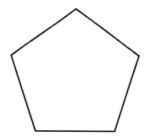

Similar polygons

Note that all congruent figures are also similar, but not all similar figures are congruent.

Review Video: <u>Polygons, Similarity, and Congruence</u>
Visit mometrix.com/academy and enter code: 686174

Line of Symmetry

A **line of symmetry** is a line that divides a figure or object into two symmetric parts. Each symmetric half is congruent to the other. An object may have no lines of symmetry, one line of symmetry, or more than one line of symmetry.

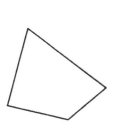 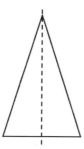 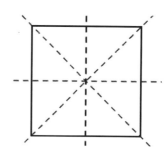

No lines of symmetry   One line of symmetry   Multiple lines of symmetry

- 5 -

Quadrilateral: A closed two-dimensional geometric figure composed of exactly four straight sides. The sum of the interior angles of any quadrilateral is 360°.

Parallelogram

A **parallelogram** is a quadrilateral that has exactly two pairs of opposite parallel sides. The sides that are parallel are also congruent. The opposite interior angles are always congruent, and the consecutive interior angles are supplementary. The diagonals of a parallelogram bisect each other. Each diagonal divides the parallelogram into two congruent triangles.

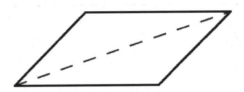

Trapezoid

Traditionally, a **trapezoid** is a quadrilateral that has exactly one pair of parallel sides. Some math texts define trapezoid as a quadrilateral that has at least one pair of parallel sides. Because there are no rules governing the second pair of sides, there are no rules that apply to the properties of the diagonals of a trapezoid.

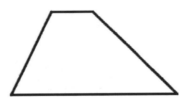

Rectangles, rhombuses, and squares are all special forms of parallelograms.

Rectangle

A **rectangle** is a parallelogram with four right angles. All rectangles are parallelograms, but not all parallelograms are rectangles. The diagonals of a rectangle are congruent.

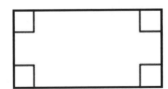

Rhombus

A **rhombus** is a parallelogram with four congruent sides. All rhombuses are parallelograms, but not all parallelograms are rhombuses. The diagonals of a rhombus are perpendicular to each other.

Review Video: Diagonals of Parallelograms, Rectangles, and Rhombi
Visit mometrix.com/academy and enter code: 320040

Square

A **square** is a parallelogram with four right angles and four congruent sides. All squares are also parallelograms, rhombuses, and rectangles. The diagonals of a square are congruent and perpendicular to each other.

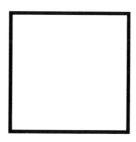

A quadrilateral whose diagonals bisect each other is a **parallelogram**. A quadrilateral whose opposite sides are parallel (2 pairs of parallel sides) is a parallelogram.

A quadrilateral whose diagonals are perpendicular bisectors of each other is a **rhombus**. A quadrilateral whose opposite sides (both pairs) are parallel and congruent is a rhombus.

A parallelogram that has a right angle is a **rectangle**. (Consecutive angles of a parallelogram are supplementary. Therefore if there is one right angle in a parallelogram, there are four right angles in that parallelogram.)

A rhombus with one right angle is a **square**. Because the rhombus is a special form of a parallelogram, the rules about the angles of a parallelogram also apply to the rhombus.

Area and Perimeter Formulas

Triangle

The *perimeter of any triangle* is found by summing the three side lengths; $P = a + b + c$. For an equilateral triangle, this is the same as $P = 3s$, where s is any side length, since all three sides are the same length.

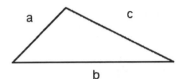

Square

The *area of a square* is found by using the formula $A = s^2$, where and s is the length of one side.

The *perimeter of a square* is found by using the formula $P = 4s$, where s is the length of one side. Because all four sides are equal in a square, it is faster to multiply the length of one side by 4 than to add the same number four times. You could use the formulas for rectangles and get the same answer.

> **Review Video: Area and Perimeter of a Square**
> Visit mometrix.com/academy and enter code: 620902

Rectangle

The *area of a rectangle* is found by the formula $A = lw$, where A is the area of the rectangle, l is the length (usually considered to be the longer side) and w is the width (usually considered to be the shorter side). The numbers for l and w are interchangeable.

The *perimeter of a rectangle* is found by the formula $P = 2l + 2w$ or $P = 2(l + w)$, where l is the length, and w is the width. It may be easier to add the length and width first and then double the result, as in the second formula.

> **Review Video: Area and Perimeter of a Rectangle**
> Visit mometrix.com/academy and enter code: 933707

Parallelogram

The *area of a parallelogram* is found by the formula $A = bh$, where b is the length of the base, and h is the height. Note that the base and height correspond to the length and width in a rectangle, so this formula would apply to rectangles as well. Do not confuse the height of a parallelogram with the length of the second side. The two are only the same measure in the case of a rectangle.

The *perimeter of a parallelogram* is found by the formula $P = 2a + 2b$ or $P = 2(a + b)$, where a and b are the lengths of the two sides.

> **Review Video: Area and Perimeter of a Parallelogram**
> Visit mometrix.com/academy and enter code: 718313

Trapezoid

The *area of a trapezoid* is found by the formula $A = \frac{1}{2}h(b_1 + b_2)$, where h is the height (segment joining and perpendicular to the parallel bases), and b_1 and b_2 are the two parallel sides (bases). Do not use one of the other two sides as the height unless that side is also perpendicular to the parallel bases.

The *perimeter of a trapezoid* is found by the formula $P = a + b_1 + c + b_2$, where a, b_1, c, and b_2 are the four sides of the trapezoid.

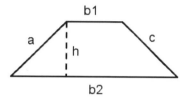

> **Review Video:** Area and Perimeter of a Trapezoid
> Visit mometrix.com/academy and enter code: 587523

Triangles

An **equilateral triangle** is a triangle with three congruent sides. An equilateral triangle will also have three congruent angles, each 60°. All equilateral triangles are also acute triangles.

An **isosceles triangle** is a triangle with two congruent sides. An isosceles triangle will also have two congruent angles opposite the two congruent sides.

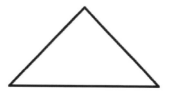

A **scalene triangle** is a triangle with no congruent sides. A scalene triangle will also have three angles of different measures. The angle with the largest measure is opposite the longest side, and the angle with the smallest measure is opposite the shortest side.

- 9 -

An **acute triangle** is a triangle whose three angles are all less than 90°. If two of the angles are equal, the acute triangle is also an isosceles triangle. If the three angles are all equal, the acute triangle is also an equilateral triangle.

A **right triangle** is a triangle with exactly one angle equal to 90°. All right triangles follow the Pythagorean theorem. A right triangle can never be acute or obtuse.

An **obtuse triangle** is a triangle with exactly one angle greater than 90°. The other two angles may or may not be equal. If the two remaining angles are equal, the obtuse triangle is also an isosceles triangle.

> **Review Video: Introduction to Types of Triangles**
> Visit mometrix.com/academy and enter code: 511711

Terminology

Altitude of a triangle

A line segment drawn from one vertex perpendicular to the opposite side. In the diagram below, $\overline{BE}$, $\overline{AD}$, and $\overline{CF}$ are altitudes. The three altitudes in a triangle are always concurrent.

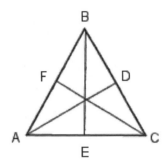

Height of a triangle

The length of the altitude, although the two terms are often used interchangeably.

Orthocenter of a triangle

The point of concurrency of the altitudes of a triangle. Note that in an obtuse triangle, the orthocenter will be outside the triangle, and in a right triangle, the orthocenter is the vertex of the right angle.

Median of a triangle

A line segment drawn from one vertex to the midpoint of the opposite side. This is not the same as the altitude, except the altitude to the base of an isosceles triangle and all three altitudes of an equilateral triangle.

Centroid of a triangle

The point of concurrency of the medians of a triangle. This is the same point as the orthocenter only in an equilateral triangle. Unlike the orthocenter, the centroid is always inside the triangle. The centroid can also be considered the exact center of the triangle. Any shape triangle can be perfectly balanced on a tip placed at the centroid. The centroid is also the point that is two-thirds the distance from the vertex to the opposite side.

Pythagorean Theorem

The side of a triangle opposite the right angle is called the **hypotenuse**. The other two sides are called the legs. The Pythagorean theorem states a relationship among the legs and hypotenuse of a right triangle: $a^2 + b^2 = c^2$, where a and b are the lengths of the legs of a right triangle, and c is the length of the hypotenuse. Note that this formula will only work with right triangles.

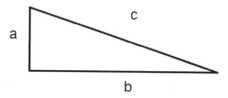

General Rules

The *triangle inequality theorem* states that the sum of the measures of any two sides of a triangle is always greater than the measure of the third side. If the sum of the measures of two sides were equal to the third side, a triangle would be impossible because the two sides would lie flat across the third side and there would be no vertex. If the sum of the measures of two of the sides was less than the third side, a closed figure would be impossible because the two shortest sides would never meet.

The sum of the measures of the interior angles of a triangle is always 180°. Therefore, a triangle can never have more than one angle greater than or equal to 90°.

In any triangle, the angles opposite congruent sides are congruent, and the sides opposite congruent angles are congruent. The largest angle is always opposite the longest side, and the smallest angle is always opposite the shortest side.

The line segment that joins the midpoints of any two sides of a triangle is always parallel to the third side and exactly half the length of the third side.

Similarity and Congruence Rules

Similar triangles are triangles whose corresponding angles are equal and whose corresponding sides are proportional. Represented by AA. Similar triangles whose corresponding sides are congruent are also congruent triangles.

Three sides of one triangle are congruent to the three corresponding sides of the second triangle. Represented as SSS.

Two sides and the included angle (the angle formed by those two sides) of one triangle are congruent to the corresponding two sides and included angle of the second triangle. Represented by SAS.

Two angles and the included side (the side that joins the two angles) of one triangle are congruent to the corresponding two angles and included side of the second triangle. Represented by ASA.

Two angles and a non-included side of one triangle are congruent to the corresponding two angles and non-included side of the second triangle. Represented by AAS.

Note that AAA is not a form for congruent triangles. This would say that the three angles are congruent, but says nothing about the sides. This meets the requirements for similar triangles, but not congruent triangles.

Area and Perimeter Formulas

The *perimeter of any triangle* is found by summing the three side lengths; $P = a + b + c$. For an equilateral triangle, this is the same as $P = 3s$, where s is any side length, since all three sides are the same length.

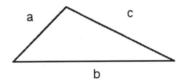

The area of any triangle can be found by taking half the product of one side length (base or b) and the perpendicular distance from that side to the opposite vertex (height or h). In equation form, $A = \frac{1}{2}bh$. For many triangles, it may be difficult to calculate h, so using one of the other formulas given here may be easier.

Another formula that works for any triangle is $A = \sqrt{s(s-a)(s-b)(s-c)}$, where A is the area, s is the semiperimeter $s = \frac{a+b+c}{2}$, and a, b, and c are the lengths of the three sides.

The area of an equilateral triangle can be found by the formula $A = \frac{\sqrt{3}}{4}s^2$, where A is the area and s is the length of a side. You could use the $30° - 60° - 90°$ ratios to find the height of the triangle and then use the standard triangle area formula, but this is faster.

The area of an isosceles triangle can be found by the formula, $A = \frac{1}{2}b\sqrt{a^2 - \frac{b^2}{4}}$, where A is the area, b is the base (the unique side), and a is the length of one of the two congruent sides. If you do not remember this formula, you can use the Pythagorean theorem to find the height so you can use the standard formula for the area of a triangle.

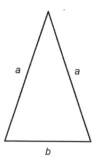

Rotation, Center of Rotation, and Angle of Rotation

A *rotation* is a transformation that turns a figure around a point called the **center of rotation**, which can lie anywhere in the plane. If a line is drawn from a point on a figure to the center of rotation, and another line is drawn from the center to the rotated image of that point, the angle between the two lines is the **angle of rotation**. The vertex of the angle of rotation is the center of rotation.

Reflection over a Line and Reflection in a Point

A reflection of a figure over a *line* (a "flip") creates a congruent image that is the same distance from the line as the original figure but on the opposite side. The **line of reflection** is the perpendicular bisector of any line segment drawn from a point on the original figure to its reflected image (unless the point and its reflected image happen to be the same point, which happens when a figure is reflected over one of its own sides).

A reflection of a figure in a *point* is the same as the rotation of the figure 180° about that point. The image of the figure is congruent to the original figure. The **point of reflection** is the midpoint of a line segment which connects a point in the figure to its image (unless the point and its reflected image happen to be the same point, which happens when a figure is reflected in one of its own points).

Use the coordinate plane of the given image below to reflect the image across the *y*-axis.

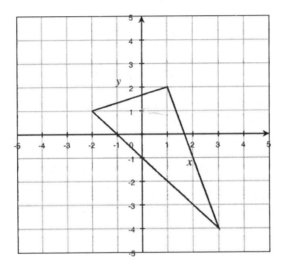

To reflect the image across the *y*-axis, replace each *x*-coordinate of the points that are the vertex of the triangle, *x*, with its negative, –*x*.

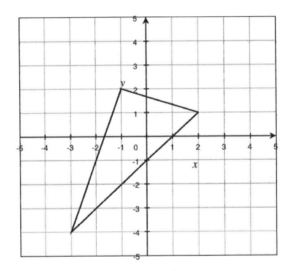

Translation

A *translation* is a transformation which slides a figure from one position in the plane to another position in the plane. The original figure and the translated figure have the same size, shape, and orientation.

> **Review Video: Translation**
> Visit mometrix.com/academy and enter code: 718628

Transforming a Given Figure Using Rotation, Reflection, and Translation

To **rotate** a given figure: 1. Identify the point of rotation. 2. Using tracing paper, geometry software, or by approximation, recreate the figure at a new location around the point of rotation.

To **reflect** a given figure: 1. Identify the line of reflection. 2. By folding the paper, using geometry software, or by approximation, recreate the image at a new location on the other side of the line of reflection.

To **translate** a given figure: 1. Identify the new location. 2. Using graph paper, geometry software, or by approximation, recreate the figure in the new location. If using graph paper, make a chart of the x- and y-values to keep track of the coordinates of all critical points.

Evidence of Transformation

To identify that a figure has been *rotated*, look for evidence that the figure is still face-up, but has changed its orientation.

To identify that a figure has been *reflected* across a line, look for evidence that the figure is now face-down.

To identify that a figure has been *translated*, look for evidence that a figure is still face-up and has not changed orientation; the only change is location.

To identify that a figure has been *dilated*, look for evidence that the figure has changed its size but not its orientation.

Dilation

A **dilation** is a transformation which proportionally stretches or shrinks a figure by a **scale factor**. The dilated image is the same shape and orientation as the original image but a different size. A polygon and its dilated image are similar.

<u>Example 1</u>

Use the coordinate plane to create a dilation of the given image below, where the dilation is the enlargement of the original image.

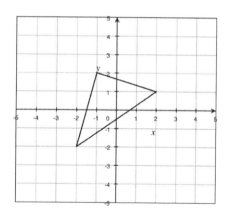

An enlargement can be found by multiplying each coordinate of the coordinate pairs located at the triangles vertices by a constant. If the figure is enlarged by a factor of 2, the new image would be:

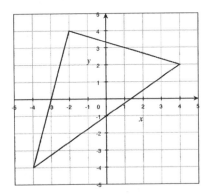

Trigonometric Formulas

In the diagram below, angle C is the **right angle**, and side c is the **hypotenuse**. Side a is the side adjacent to angle B and side b is the side adjacent to angle A. These formulas will work for any acute angle in a right triangle. They will *not* work for any triangle that is not a right triangle. Also, they will not work for the right angle in a right triangle, since there are not distinct adjacent and opposite sides to differentiate from the hypotenuse.

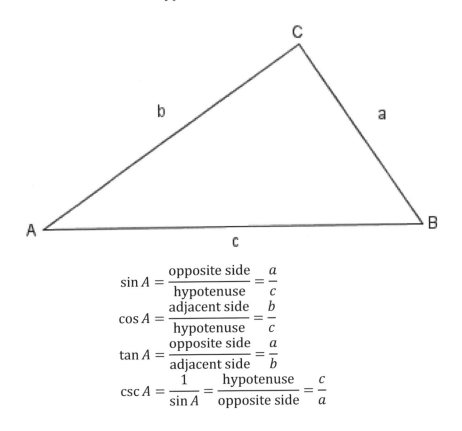

$$\sin A = \frac{\text{opposite side}}{\text{hypotenuse}} = \frac{a}{c}$$

$$\cos A = \frac{\text{adjacent side}}{\text{hypotenuse}} = \frac{b}{c}$$

$$\tan A = \frac{\text{opposite side}}{\text{adjacent side}} = \frac{a}{b}$$

$$\csc A = \frac{1}{\sin A} = \frac{\text{hypotenuse}}{\text{opposite side}} = \frac{c}{a}$$

$$\sec A = \frac{1}{\cos A} = \frac{\text{hypotenuse}}{\text{adjacent side}} = \frac{c}{b}$$

$$\cot A = \frac{1}{\tan A} = \frac{\text{adjacent side}}{\text{opposite side}} = \frac{b}{a}$$

Laws of Sines and Cosines

The **law of sines** states that $\frac{\sin A}{a} = \frac{\sin B}{b} = \frac{\sin C}{c}$, where A, B, and C are the angles of a triangle, and a, b, and c are the sides opposite their respective angles. This formula will work with all triangles, not just right triangles.

The **law of cosines** is given by the formula $c^2 = a^2 + b^2 - 2ab(\cos C)$, where a, b, and c are the sides of a triangle, and C is the angle opposite side c. This formula is similar to the *pythagorean theorem*, but unlike the pythagorean theorem, it can be used on any triangle.

> **Review Video: Cosine**
> Visit mometrix.com/academy and enter code: 361120

Circles

The **center** is the single point inside the circle that is **equidistant** from every point on the circle. (Point O in the diagram below.)

> **Review Video: Points of a Circle**
> Visit mometrix.com/academy and enter code: 420746

The **radius** is a line segment that joins the center of the circle and any one point on the circle. All radii of a circle are equal. (Segments OX, OY, and OZ in the diagram below.)

The **diameter** is a line segment that passes through the center of the circle and has both endpoints on the circle. The length of the diameter is exactly twice the length of the radius. (Segment XZ in the diagram below.)

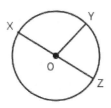

The **area of a circle** is found by the formula $A = \pi r^2$, where r is the length of the radius. If the diameter of the circle is given, remember to divide it in half to get the length of the radius before proceeding.

> **Review Video: The Diameter, Radius, and Circumference of Circles**
> Visit mometrix.com/academy and enter code: 448988

- 17 -

The **circumference** of a circle is found by the formula $C = 2\pi r$, where r is the radius. Again, remember to convert the diameter if you are given that measure rather than the radius.

Concentric circles are circles that have the same center, but not the same length of radii. A bulls-eye target is an example of concentric circles.

An **arc** is a portion of a circle. Specifically, an arc is the set of points between and including two points on a circle. An arc does not contain any points inside the circle. When a segment is drawn from the endpoints of an arc to the center of the circle, a sector is formed.

A **central angle** is an angle whose vertex is the center of a circle and whose legs intercept an arc of the circle. Angle XOY in the diagram above is a central angle. A minor arc is an arc that has a measure less than 180°. The measure of a central angle is equal to the measure of the minor arc it intercepts. A major arc is an arc having a measure of at least 180°. The measure of the major arc can be found by subtracting the measure of the central angle from 360°.

A **semicircle** is an arc whose endpoints are the endpoints of the diameter of a circle. A semicircle is exactly half of a circle.

An **inscribed angle** is an angle whose vertex lies on a circle and whose legs contain chords of that circle. The portion of the circle intercepted by the legs of the angle is called the intercepted arc. The measure of the intercepted arc is exactly twice the measure of the inscribed angle. In the following diagram, angle ABC is an inscribed angle. $\overset{\frown}{AC} = 2(\text{m}\angle ABC)$

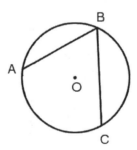

Any angle inscribed in a semicircle is a right angle. The intercepted arc is 180°, making the inscribed angle half that, or 90°. In the diagram below, angle ABC is inscribed in semicircle ABC, making angle ABC equal to 90°.

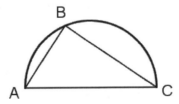

A **chord** is a line segment that has both endpoints on a circle. In the diagram below, $\overline{EB}$ is a chord.

Secant: A line that passes through a circle and contains a chord of that circle. In the diagram below, $\overleftrightarrow{EB}$ is a secant and contains chord $\overline{EB}$.

A **tangent** is a line in the same plane as a circle that touches the circle in exactly one point. While a line segment can be tangent to a circle as part of a line that is tangent, it is improper to say a tangent can be simply a line segment that touches the circle in exactly one point. In the diagram below, $\overleftrightarrow{CD}$ is tangent to circle A. Notice that $\overline{FB}$ is not tangent to the circle. $\overline{FB}$ is a line segment that touches the circle in exactly one point, but if the segment were extended, it would touch the circle in a second point. The point at which a tangent touches a circle is called the point of tangency. In the diagram below, point B is the point of tangency.

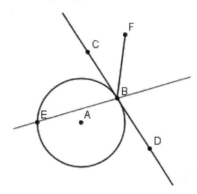

A **secant** is a line that intersects a circle in two points. Two secants may intersect inside the circle, on the circle, or outside the circle. When the two secants intersect on the circle, an inscribed angle is formed.

When two secants intersect inside a circle, the measure of each of two vertical angles is equal to half the sum of the two intercepted arcs. In the diagram below, m$\angle AEB = \frac{1}{2}(\widehat{AB} + \widehat{CD})$ and m$\angle BEC = \frac{1}{2}(\widehat{BC} + \widehat{AD})$.

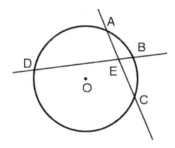

When two secants intersect outside a circle, the measure of the angle formed is equal to half the difference of the two arcs that lie between the two secants. In the diagram below, m∠AEB = $\frac{1}{2}(\overarc{AB} - \overarc{CD})$.

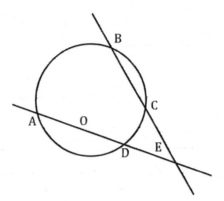

The **arc length** is the length of that portion of the circumference between two points on the circle. The formula for arc length is $s = \frac{\pi r \theta}{180°}$ where s is the arc length, r is the length of the radius, and θ is the angular measure of the arc in degrees, or $s = r\theta$, where θ is the angular measure of the arc in radians (2π radians = 360 degrees).

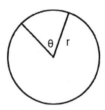

A **sector** is the portion of a circle formed by two radii and their intercepted arc. While the arc length is exclusively the points that are also on the circumference of the circle, the sector is the entire area bounded by the arc and the two radii.

The **area of a sector** of a circle is found by the formula, $A = \frac{\theta r^2}{2}$, where A is the area, θ is the measure of the central angle in radians, and r is the radius. To find the area when the central angle is in degrees, use the formula, $A = \frac{\theta \pi r^2}{360}$, where θ is the measure of the central angle in degrees and r is the radius.

A circle is inscribed in a polygon if each of the sides of the polygon is tangent to the circle. A polygon is inscribed in a circle if each of the vertices of the polygon lies on the circle.

A circle is circumscribed about a polygon if each of the vertices of the polygon lies on the circle. A polygon is circumscribed about the circle if each of the sides of the polygon is tangent to the circle.

If one figure is inscribed in another, then the other figure is circumscribed about the first figure.

Circle circumscribed about a pentagon
Pentagon inscribed in a circle

Other Conic Sections

Ellipse

An **ellipse** is the set of all points in a plane, whose total distance from two fixed points called the foci (singular: focus) is constant, and whose center is the midpoint between the foci.

The standard equation of an ellipse that is taller than it is wide is $\frac{(y-k)^2}{a^2} + \frac{(x-h)^2}{b^2} = 1$, where a and b are coefficients. The center is the point (h, k) and the foci are the points $(h, k + c)$ and $(h, k - c)$, where $c^2 = a^2 - b^2$ and $a^2 > b^2$.

The major axis has length $2a$, and the minor axis has length $2b$.

Eccentricity (e) is a measure of how elongated an ellipse is, and is the ratio of the distance between the foci to the length of the major axis. Eccentricity will have a value between 0 and 1. The closer to 1 the eccentricity is, the closer the ellipse is to being a circle. The formula for eccentricity is $= \frac{c}{a}$.

Parabola

Parabola: The set of all points in a plane that are equidistant from a fixed line, called the **directrix**, and a fixed point not on the line, called the **focus**.

Axis: The line perpendicular to the directrix that passes through the focus.

For parabolas that open up or down, the standard equation is $(x - h)^2 = 4c(y - k)$, where h, c, and k are coefficients. If c is positive, the parabola opens up. If c is negative, the parabola opens down. The vertex is the point (h, k). The directrix is the line having the equation $y = -c + k$, and the focus is the point $(h, c + k)$.

For parabolas that open left or right, the standard equation is $(y - k)^2 = 4c(x - h)$, where k, c, and h are coefficients. If c is positive, the parabola opens to the right. If c is negative, the parabola opens to the left. The vertex is the point (h, k). The directrix is the line having the equation $x = -c + h$, and the focus is the point $(c + h, k)$.

Hyperbola

A **hyperbola** is the set of all points in a plane, whose distance from two fixed points, called foci, has a constant difference.

The standard equation of a horizontal hyperbola is $\frac{(x-h)^2}{a^2} - \frac{(y-k)^2}{b^2} = 1$, where a, b, h, and k are real numbers. The center is the point (h, k), the vertices are the points $(h + a, k)$ and $(h - a, k)$, and the foci are the points that every point on one of the parabolic curves is equidistant from and are found using the formulas $(h + c, k)$ and $(h - c, k)$, where $c^2 = a^2 + b^2$. The asymptotes are two lines the graph of the hyperbola approaches but never reaches, and are given by the equations $y = \left(\frac{b}{a}\right)(x - h) + k$ and $y = -\left(\frac{b}{a}\right)(x - h) + k$.

A **vertical hyperbola** is formed when a plane makes a vertical cut through two cones that are stacked vertex-to-vertex.

The standard equation of a vertical hyperbola is $\frac{(y-k)^2}{a^2} - \frac{(x-h)^2}{b^2} = 1$, where a, b, k, and h are real numbers. The center is the point (h, k), the vertices are the points $(h, k + a)$ and $(h, k - a)$, and the foci are the points that every point on one of the parabolic curves is equidistant from and are found using the formulas $(h, k + c)$ and $(h, k - c)$, where $c^2 = a^2 + b^2$. The asymptotes are two lines the graph of the hyperbola approaches but never reach, and are given by the equations $y = \left(\frac{a}{b}\right)(x - h) + k$ and $y = -\left(\frac{a}{b}\right)(x - h) + k$.

Solids

The **surface area of a solid object** is the area of all sides or exterior surfaces. For objects such as prisms and pyramids, a further distinction is made between base surface area (B) and lateral surface area (LA). For a prism, the total surface area (SA) is $SA = LA + 2B$. For a pyramid or cone, the total surface area is $SA = LA + B$.

> **Review Video: How to Calculate the Volume of 3D Objects**
> Visit mometrix.com/academy and enter code: 163343

The **surface area of a sphere** can be found by the formula $A = 4\pi r^2$, where r is the radius. The volume is given by the formula $V = \frac{4}{3}\pi r^3$, where r is the radius. Both quantities are generally given in terms of π.

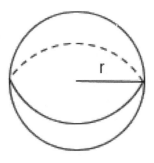

> **Review Video: Volume and Surface Area of a Sphere**
> Visit mometrix.com/academy and enter code: 786928

The **volume of any prism** is found by the formula $V = Bh$, where B is the area of the base, and h is the height (perpendicular distance between the bases). The surface area of any prism is the sum of the areas of both bases and all sides. It can be calculated as $SA = 2B + Ph$, where P is the perimeter of the base.

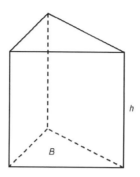

For a *rectangular prism*, the **volume** can be found by the formula $V = lwh$, where V is the volume, l is the length, w is the width, and h is the height. The surface area can be calculated as $SA = 2lw + 2hl + 2wh$ or $SA = 2(lw + hl + wh)$.

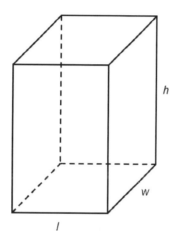

The **volume of a cube** can be found by the formula $V = s^3$, where s is the length of a side. The surface area of a cube is calculated as $SA = 6s^2$, where SA is the total surface area and s is the length of a side. These formulas are the same as the ones used for the volume and surface area of a rectangular prism, but simplified since all three quantities (length, width, and height) are the same.

> **Review Video: Volume and Surface Area of a Cube**
> Visit mometrix.com/academy and enter code: 664455

The **volume of a cylinder** can be calculated by the formula $V = \pi r^2 h$, where r is the radius, and h is the height. The surface area of a cylinder can be found by the formula $SA = 2\pi r^2 + 2\pi rh$. The first term is the base area multiplied by two, and the second term is the perimeter of the base multiplied by the height.

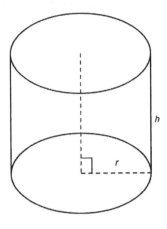

The **volume of a pyramid** is found by the formula $V = \frac{1}{3}Bh$, where B is the area of the base, and h is the height (perpendicular distance from the vertex to the base). Notice this formula is the same as $\frac{1}{3}$ times the volume of a prism. Like a prism, the base of a pyramid can be any shape.

Finding the **surface area of a pyramid** is not as simple as the other shapes we've looked at thus far. If the pyramid is a right pyramid, meaning the base is a regular polygon and the vertex is directly over the center of that polygon, the surface area can be calculated as $SA = B + \frac{1}{2}Ph_s$, where P is the perimeter of the base, and h_s is the slant height (distance from the vertex to the midpoint of one side of the base). If the pyramid is irregular, the area of each triangle side must be calculated individually and then summed, along with the base.

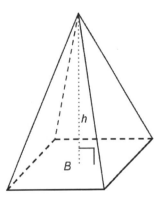

The **volume of a cone** is found by the formula $V = \frac{1}{3}\pi r^2 h$, where r is the radius, and h is the height. Notice this is the same as $\frac{1}{3}$ times the volume of a cylinder. The surface area can be calculated as

- 24 -

$SA = \pi r^2 + \pi r s$, where s is the slant height. The slant height can be calculated using the Pythagorean Thereom to be $\sqrt{r^2 + h^2}$, so the surface area formula can also be written as $SA = \pi r^2 + \pi r\sqrt{r^2 + h^2}$.

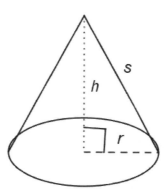

Probability

Probability Terminology

Probability is a branch of statistics that deals with the likelihood of something taking place. One classic example is a coin toss. There are only two possible results: heads or tails. The likelihood, or probability, that the coin will land as heads is 1 out of 2 ($\frac{1}{2}$, 0.5, 50%). Tails has the same probability. Another common example is a 6-sided die roll. There are six possible results from rolling a single die, each with an equal chance of happening, so the probability of any given number coming up is 1 out of 6.

<u>Terms frequently used in probability</u>

- **Event** – a situation that produces results of some sort (a coin toss)
- **Compound event** – event that involves two or more independent events (rolling a pair of dice; taking the sum)
- **Outcome** – a possible result in an experiment or event (heads, tails)
- **Desired outcome** (or success) – an outcome that meets a particular set of criteria (a roll of 1 or 2 if we are looking for numbers less than 3)
- **Independent events** – two or more events whose outcomes do not affect one another (two coins tossed at the same time)
- **Dependent events** – two or more events whose outcomes affect one another (two cards drawn consecutively from the same deck)
- **Certain outcome** – probability of outcome is 100% or 1
- **Impossible outcome** – probability of outcome is 0% or 0
- **Mutually exclusive outcomes** – two or more outcomes whose criteria cannot all be satisfied in a single event (a coin coming up heads and tails on the same toss)

Calculating Probability

Probability is the likelihood of a certain outcome occurring for a given event. The **theoretical probability** can usually be determined without actually performing the event. The likelihood of a outcome occurring, or the probability of an outcome occurring, is given by the formula

$$P(A) = \frac{\text{Number of acceptable outcomes}}{\text{Number of possible outcomes}}$$

where $P(A)$ is the probability of an outcome A occurring, and each outcome is just as likely to occur as any other outcome. If each outcome has the same probability of occurring as every other possible outcome, the outcomes are said to be equally likely to occur. The total number of acceptable outcomes must be less than or equal to the total number of possible outcomes. If the two are equal, then the outcome is certain to occur and the probability is 1. If the number of acceptable outcomes is zero, then the outcome is impossible and the probability is 0.

> **Review Video: Theoretical and Experimental Probability**
> Visit mometrix.com/academy and enter code: 444349

Example:

There are 20 marbles in a bag and 5 are red. The theoretical probability of randomly selecting a red marble is 5 out of 20, ($\frac{5}{20} = \frac{1}{4}$, 0.25, or 25%).

Permutations and Combinations

When trying to calculate the probability of an event using the $\frac{\text{desired outcomes}}{\text{total outcomes}}$ formula, you may frequently find that there are too many outcomes to individually count them. **Permutation** and **combination formulas** offer a shortcut to counting outcomes. A permutation is an arrangement of a specific number of a set of objects in a specific order. The number of **permutations** of r items given a set of n items can be calculated as $_nP_r = \frac{n!}{(n-r)!}$. Combinations are similar to permutations, except there are no restrictions regarding the order of the elements. While ABC is considered a different permutation than BCA, ABC and BCA are considered the same combination. The number of **combinations** of r items given a set of n items can be calculated as $_nC_r = \frac{n!}{r!(n-r)!}$ or $_nC_r = \frac{_nP_r}{r!}$.

Example:

Suppose you want to calculate how many different 5-card hands can be drawn from a deck of 52 cards. This is a combination since the order of the cards in a hand does not matter. There are 52 cards available, and 5 to be selected. Thus, the number of different hands is $_{52}C_5 = \frac{52!}{5! \times 47!} = 2{,}598{,}960$.

Complement of an Event

Sometimes it may be easier to calculate the possibility of something not happening, or the **complement of an event**. Represented by the symbol $\bar{A}$, the complement of A is the probability that event A does not happen. When you know the probability of event A occurring, you can use the formula $P(\bar{A}) = 1 - P(A)$, where $P(\bar{A})$ is the probability of event A not occurring, and $P(A)$ is the probability of event A occurring.

- 26 -

Addition Rule

The **addition rule** for probability is used for finding the probability of a compound event. Use the formula $P(A \text{ or } B) = P(A) + P(B) - P(A \text{ and } B)$, where $P(A \text{ and } B)$ is the probability of both events occurring to find the probability of a compound event. The probability of both events occurring at the same time must be subtracted to eliminate any overlap in the first two probabilities.

Conditional Probability

Conditional probability is the probability of an event occurring once another event has already occurred. Given event A and dependent event B, the probability of event B occurring when event A has already occurred is represented by the notation $P(A|B)$. To find the probability of event B occurring, take into account the fact that event A has already occurred and adjust the total number of possible outcomes. For example, suppose you have ten balls numbered 1–10 and you want ball number 7 to be pulled in two pulls. On the first pull, the probability of getting the 7 is $\frac{1}{10}$ because there is one ball with a 7 on it and 10 balls to choose from. Assuming the first pull did not yield a 7, the probability of pulling a 7 on the second pull is now $\frac{1}{9}$ because there are only 9 balls remaining for the second pull.

Multiplication Rule

The **multiplication rule** can be used to find the probability of two independent events occurring using the formula $P(A \text{ and } B) = P(A) \times P(B)$, where $P(A \text{ and } B)$ is the probability of two independent events occurring, $P(A)$ is the probability of the first event occurring, and $P(B)$ is the probability of the second event occurring.

The multiplication rule can also be used to find the probability of two dependent events occurring using the formula $P(A \text{ and } B) = P(A) \times P(B|A)$, where $P(A \text{ and } B)$ is the probability of two dependent events occurring and $P(B|A)$ is the probability of the second event occurring after the first event has already occurred.

Before using the multiplication rule, you MUST first determine whether the two events are *dependent* or *independent*.

Use a **combination of the multiplication** rule and the rule of complements to find the probability that at least one outcome of the element will occur. This given by the general formula $P(\text{at least one event occurring}) = 1 - P(\text{no outcomes occurring})$. For example, to find the probability that at least one even number will show when a pair of dice is rolled, find the probability that two odd numbers will be rolled (no even numbers) and subtract from one. You can always use a tree diagram or make a chart to list the possible outcomes when the sample space is small, such as in the dice-rolling example, but in most cases it will be much faster to use the multiplication and complement formulas.

Expected Value

Expected value is a method of determining expected outcome in a random situation. It is really a sum of the weighted probabilities of the possible outcomes. Multiply the probability of an event occurring by the weight assigned to that probability (such as the amount of money won or lost). A practical application of the expected value is to determine whether a game of chance is really fair. If the sum of the weighted probabilities is equal to zero, the game is generally considered fair because the player has a fair chance to at least to break even. If the expected value is less than zero, then players lose more than they win. For example, a lottery drawing might allow the player to choose any three-digit number, 000–999. The probability of choosing the winning number is 1:1000. If it

- 27 -

costs \$1 to play, and a winning number receives \$500, the expected value is $\left(-\$1 \cdot \frac{999}{1,000}\right) +$ $\left(\$500 \cdot \frac{1}{1,000}\right) = -0.499$ or $-\$0.50$. You can expect to lose on average 50 cents for every dollar you spend.

Empirical Probability

Most of the time, when we talk about probability, we mean theoretical probability. **Empirical probability**, or experimental probability or relative frequency, is the number of times an outcome occurs in a particular experiment or a certain number of observed events. While theoretical probability is based on what *should* happen, experimental probability is based on what *has* happened. Experimental probability is calculated in the same way as theoretical, except that actual outcomes are used instead of possible outcomes.

Theoretical and experimental probability do not always line up with one another. Theoretical probability says that out of 20 coin-tosses, 10 should be heads. However, if we were actually to toss 20 coins, we might record just 5 heads. This doesn't mean that our theoretical probability is incorrect; it just means that this particular experiment had results that were different from what was predicted. A practical application of empirical probability is the insurance industry. There are no set functions that define lifespan, health, or safety. Insurance companies look at factors from hundreds of thousands of individuals to find patterns that they then use to set the formulas for insurance premiums.

Objective Probability

Objective probability is based on mathematical formulas and documented evidence. Examples of objective probability include raffles or lottery drawings where there is a pre-determined number of possible outcomes and a predetermined number of outcomes that correspond to an event. Other cases of objective probability include probabilities of rolling dice, flipping coins, or drawing cards. Most gambling games are based on objective probability.

Subjective Probability

Subjective probability is based on personal or professional feelings and judgments. Often, there is a lot of guesswork following extensive research. Areas where subjective probability is applicable include sales trends and business expenses. Attractions set admission prices based on subjective probabilities of attendance based on varying admission rates in an effort to maximize their profit.

Sample Space

The total set of all possible results of a test or experiment is called a **sample space**, or sometimes a universal sample space. The sample space, represented by one of the variables S, Ω, or U (for universal sample space) has individual elements called outcomes. Other terms for outcome that may be used interchangeably include elementary outcome, simple event, or sample point. The number of outcomes in a given sample space could be infinite or finite, and some tests may yield multiple unique sample sets. For example, tests conducted by drawing playing cards from a standard deck would have one sample space of the card values, another sample space of the card suits, and a third sample space of suit-denomination combinations. For most tests, the sample spaces considered will be finite.

An **event**, represented by the variable E, is a portion of a sample space. It may be one outcome or a group of outcomes from the same sample space. If an event occurs, then the test or experiment will generate an outcome that satisfies the requirement of that event. For example, given a standard deck of 52 playing cards as the sample space, and defining the event as the collection of face cards, then the event will occur if the card drawn is a J, Q, or K. If any other card is drawn, the event is said to have not occurred.

For every sample space, each possible outcome has a specific likelihood, or probability, that it will occur. The probability measure, also called the **distribution**, is a function that assigns a real number probability, from zero to one, to each outcome. For a probability measure to be accurate, every outcome must have a real number probability measure that is greater than or equal to zero and less than or equal to one. Also, the probability measure of the sample space must equal one, and the probability measure of the union of multiple outcomes must equal the sum of the individual probability measures.

Probabilities of events are expressed as real numbers from zero to one. They give a numerical value to the chance that a particular event will occur. The probability of an event occurring is the sum of the probabilities of the individual elements of that event. For example, in a standard deck of 52 playing cards as the sample space and the collection of face cards as the event, the probability of drawing a specific face card is $\frac{1}{52} = 0.019$, but the probability of drawing any one of the twelve face cards is $12(0.019) = 0.228$. Note that rounding of numbers can generate different results. If you multiplied 12 by the fraction $\frac{1}{52}$ before converting to a decimal, you would get the answer $\frac{12}{52} = 0.231$.

Tree Diagram

For a simple sample space, possible outcomes may be determined by using a **tree diagram** or an organized chart. In either case, you can easily draw or list out the possible outcomes. For example, to determine all the possible ways three objects can be ordered, you can draw a tree diagram:

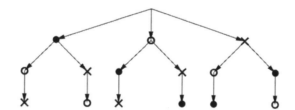

You can also make a chart to list all the possibilities:

First object	Second object	Third object
●	X	O
●	O	X
O	●	X
O	X	●
X	●	O
X	O	●

Either way, you can easily see there are six possible ways the three objects can be ordered.

If two events have no outcomes in common, they are said to be **mutually exclusive**. For example, in a standard deck of 52 playing cards, the event of all card suits is mutually exclusive to the event of all card values. If two events have no bearing on each other so that one event occurring has no influence on the probability of another event occurring, the two events are said to be independent. For example, rolling a standard six-sided die multiple times does not change that probability that a particular number will be rolled from one roll to the next. If the outcome of one event does affect the probability of the second event, the two events are said to be dependent. For example, if cards are drawn from a deck, the probability of drawing an ace after an ace has been drawn is different than the probability of drawing an ace if no ace (or no other card, for that matter) has been drawn.

In probability, the **odds in favor of an event** are the number of times the event will occur compared to the number of times the event will not occur. To calculate the odds in favor of an event, use the formula $\frac{P(A)}{1-P(A)}$, where $P(A)$ is the probability that the event will occur. Many times, odds in favor is given as a ratio in the form $\frac{a}{b}$ or $a:b$, where a is the probability of the event occurring and b is the complement of the event, the probability of the event not occurring. If the odds in favor are given as 2:5, that means that you can expect the event to occur two times for every 5 times that it does not occur. In other words, the probability that the event will occur is $\frac{2}{2+5} = \frac{2}{7}$.

In probability, the **odds against an event** are the number of times the event will not occur compared to the number of times the event will occur. To calculate the odds against an event, use the formula $\frac{1-P(A)}{P(A)}$, where $P(A)$ is the probability that the event will occur. Many times, odds against is given as a ratio in the form $\frac{b}{a}$ or $b:a$, where b is the probability the event will not occur (the complement of the event) and a is the probability the event will occur. If the odds against an event are given as 3:1, that means that you can expect the event to not occur 3 times for every one time it does occur. In other words, 3 out of every 4 trials will fail.

Experimental and Theoretical Probability

Probability, P(A), is the likelihood that event A will occur. Probability is often expressed as the ratio of ways an event can occur to the total number of **outcomes**, also called the **sample space**. For example, the probability of flipping heads on a two-sided coin can be written as $\frac{1}{2}$ since there is one side with heads and a total of two sides, which means that there are two possible outcomes. Probabilities can also be expressed as decimals or percentages.

Tree diagrams are used to list all possible outcomes. Suppose you are packing for vacation and have set aside 4 shirts, 3 pairs of pants, and 2 hats. How many possible outfits are there? To construct a tree diagram, start with the first group of events, the shirts. You can use letters to label each of the articles (SA refers to the first shirt, SB refers to the second shirt, and so on). Then, from each shirt draw branches to each pair of pants that it could be paired with. Next, from each pair of pants, draw a branch to each hat that it could be paired to and finally, repeat the process with the shoes. This method allows you to list all of the possible outcomes.

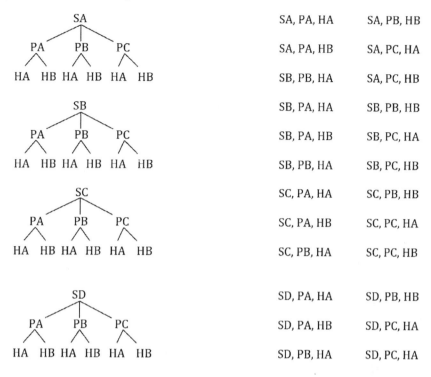

SA, PA, HA	SA, PB, HB
SA, PA, HB	SA, PC, HA
SB, PB, HA	SA, PC, HB
SB, PA, HA	SB, PB, HB
SB, PA, HB	SB, PC, HA
SB, PB, HA	SB, PC, HB
SC, PA, HA	SC, PB, HB
SC, PA, HB	SC, PC, HA
SC, PB, HA	SC, PC, HB
SD, PA, HA	SD, PB, HB
SD, PA, HB	SD, PC, HA
SD, PB, HA	SD, PC, HA

Altogether, there are 24 different combinations of shirts, pants, and hats.

A faster way to find the sample space without listing each individual outcome employs the **multiplication counting principle**. If one event can occur in a ways and a second event in b ways, then the two events can occur in $a \times b$ ways. In the previous example, there are 4 possible shirts, 3 possible pairs of pants, and 2 possible hats, so the possible number of combinations is $4 \times 3 \times 2$, or 24.

A similar principle is employed to determine the probability of two **independent events**. $P(A \text{ and } B) = P(A) \times P(B)$, where A is the first event and B is the second such that the outcome of B does not depend on the outcome of A. For instance, suppose you choose a marble from a bag of 2 red marbles, 7 blue marbles, and 4 green marbles. The probability that you would choose a red marble, replace it, and then choose a green marble is found by multiplying the probabilities of each independent event:

$$\frac{2}{13} \times \frac{4}{13} = \frac{8}{169}, \text{ or } 0.047, \text{ or } 4.7\%$$

This method can also be used when finding the probability of more than 2 independent events.

When two events are dependent on one another, the likelihood of the second event is affected by the outcome of the first event. This formula for finding the probability of **dependent events** is $P(A \text{ then } B) = P(A) \times P(B \text{ after } A)$. The probability that you choose a 2 and then choose a 5 from a deck of 52 cards without replacement is

$$\frac{4}{52} \times \frac{4}{51} = \frac{1}{13} \times \frac{4}{51} = \frac{4}{663} \text{ or } 0.0060, \text{ or } 0.60\%$$

Note that there are four of each number in a deck of cards, so the probability of choosing a 2 is $\frac{4}{52}$. Since you keep this card out of the deck, there are only 51 cards to choose from when selecting a 5.

Thus far, the discussion of probability has been limited to **theoretical probability, which is used to predict the likelihood of an event.** **Experimental probability** expresses the ratio of the number of times an event actually occurs to the number of **trials** performed in an experiment. Theoretically, the probability of rolling a one on an unloaded, six-sided die is $\frac{1}{6}$. Suppose you conduct an experiment to determine whether a dice is a fair one and obtain these results.

Trial #	1	2	3	4	5	6	7	8	9	10	11	12	13	14	15	16	17	18	19	20
Outcome	6	1	2	6	4	2	1	3	4	5	4	1	6	6	4	5	6	4	1	6

Out of the 20 trials, you rolled a 1 six times. $\frac{6}{20} = \frac{3}{10} = 0.30$, or 30%. This probability is different than the theoretical probability of $\frac{1}{6}$ or 16.6%. You might conclude that the die is loaded, but it would be advisable to conduct more trials to verify your conclusion: the larger the number of trials, the more accurate the experimental probability.

Statistics

Statistics Terminology

Statistics is the branch of mathematics that deals with collecting, recording, interpreting, illustrating, and analyzing large amounts of **data**. The following terms are often used in the discussion of data and **statistics**:

- **Data** – the collective name for pieces of *information* (singular is datum).
- **Quantitative data** – measurements (such as length, mass, and speed) that provide information about *quantities* in numbers
- **Qualitative data** – information (such as colors, scents, tastes, and shapes) that *cannot be measured* using numbers
- **Discrete data** – information that can be expressed only by a *specific value*, such as whole or half numbers. For example, since people can be counted only in whole numbers, a population count would be discrete data.
- **Continuous data** – information (such as time and temperature) that can be expressed by *any value within a given range*
- **Primary data** – information that has been *collected* directly from a survey, investigation, or experiment, such as a questionnaire or the recording of daily temperatures. Primary data that has not yet been organized or analyzed is called raw data.
- **Secondary data** – information that has been collected, sorted, and *processed* by the researcher
- **Ordinal data** – information that *can be placed in numerical order*, such as age or weight
- **Nominal data** – information that *cannot be placed in numerical order*, such as names or places.

Statistics

Population

In statistics, the **population** is the entire collection of people, plants, etc., that data can be collected from. For example, a study to determine how well students in the area schools perform on a standardized test would have a population of all the students enrolled in those schools, although a study may include just a small sample of students from each school. A **parameter** is a numerical value that gives information about the population, such as the mean, median, mode, or standard deviation. Remember that the symbol for the mean of a population is μ and the symbol for the standard deviation of a population is σ.

Sample

A **sample** is a portion of the entire population. Whereas a parameter helped describe the population, a **statistic** is a numerical value that gives information about the sample, such as mean, median, mode, or standard deviation. Keep in mind that the symbols for mean and standard deviation are different when they are referring to a sample rather than the entire population. For a sample, the symbol for mean is $\bar{x}$ and the symbol for standard deviation is s. The mean and standard deviation of a sample may or may not be identical to that of the entire population due to a sample only being a subset of the population. However, if the sample is random and large enough, statistically significant values can be attained. Samples are generally used when the population is too large to justify including every element or when acquiring data for the entire population is impossible.

Inferential Statistics

Inferential statistics is the branch of statistics that uses samples to make predictions about an entire population. This type of statistics is often seen in political polls, where a sample of the population is questioned about a particular topic or politician to gain an understanding about the attitudes of the entire population of the country. Often, exit polls are conducted on election days using this method. Inferential statistics can have a large margin of error if you do not have a valid sample.

Sampling Distribution

Statistical values calculated from various samples of the same size make up the **sampling distribution**. For example, if several samples of identical size are randomly selected from a large population and then the mean of each sample is calculated, the distribution of values of the means would be a sampling distribution.

The **sampling distribution of the mean** is the distribution of the sample mean, $\bar{x}$, derived from random samples of a given size. It has three important characteristics. First, the mean of the sampling distribution of the mean is equal to the mean of the population that was sampled. Second, assuming the standard deviation is non-zero, the standard deviation of the sampling distribution of the mean equals the standard deviation of the sampled population divided by the square root of the sample size. This is sometimes called the standard error. Finally, as the sample size gets larger, the sampling distribution of the mean gets closer to a normal distribution via the Central Limit Theorem.

Survey Study

A **survey study** is a method of gathering information from a small group in an attempt to gain enough information to make accurate general assumptions about the population. Once a survey study is completed, the results are then put into a summary report.

Survey studies are generally in the format of surveys, interviews, or questionnaires as part of an effort to find opinions of a particular group or to find facts about a group.

It is important to note that the findings from a survey study are only as accurate as the sample chosen from the population.

Correlational Studies

Correlational studies seek to determine how much one variable is affected by changes in a second variable. For example, correlational studies may look for a relationship between the amount of time a student spends studying for a test and the grade that student earned on the test or between student scores on college admissions tests and student grades in college.

It is important to note that correlational studies cannot show a cause and effect, but rather can show only that two variables are or are not potentially correlated.

Experimental Studies

Experimental studies take correlational studies one step farther, in that they attempt to prove or disprove a cause-and-effect relationship. These studies are performed by conducting a series of experiments to test the hypothesis. For a study to be scientifically accurate, it must have both an experimental group that receives the specified treatment and a control group that does not get the treatment. This is the type of study pharmaceutical companies do as part of drug trials for new medications. Experimental studies are only valid when proper scientific method has been followed. In other words, the experiment must be well-planned and executed without bias in the testing process, all subjects must be selected at random, and the process of determining which subject is in which of the two groups must also be completely random.

Observational Studies

Observational studies are the opposite of experimental studies. In observational studies, the tester cannot change or in any way control all of the variables in the test. For example, a study to determine which gender does better in math classes in school is strictly observational. You cannot change a person's gender, and you cannot change the subject being studied. The big downfall of observational studies is that you have no way of proving a cause-and-effect relationship because you cannot control outside influences. Events outside of school can influence a student's performance in school, and observational studies cannot take that into consideration.

Random Samples

For most studies, a **random sample** is necessary to produce valid results. Random samples should not have any particular influence to cause sampled subjects to behave one way or another. The goal is for the random sample to be a **representative sample**, or a sample whose characteristics give an accurate picture of the characteristics of the entire population. To accomplish this, you must make sure you have a proper **sample size**, or an appropriate number of elements in the sample.

Biases

In statistical studies, biases must be avoided. **Bias** is an error that causes the study to favor one set of results over another. For example, if a survey to determine how the country views the president's job performance only speaks to registered voters in the president's party, the results will be skewed because a disproportionately large number of responders would tend to show approval, while a disproportionately large number of people in the opposite party would tend to express disapproval.

Extraneous Variables

Extraneous variables are, as the name implies, outside influences that can affect the outcome of a study. They are not always avoidable, but could trigger bias in the result.

Data Organization

Example

A nurse found the heart rates of ten different patients to be 76, 80, 90, 86, 70, 76, 72, 88, 88, and 68 beats per minute. Organize this information in a table.

There are several ways to organize data in a table. The table below is an example.

Patient Number	1	2	3	4	5	6	7	8	9	10
Heart Rate (bpm)	76	80	90	86	70	76	72	88	88	68

When making a table, be sure to label the columns and rows appropriately.

Data Analysis

Measures of Central Tendency

The **measure of central tendency** is a statistical value that gives a general tendency for the center of a group of data. There are several different ways of describing the measure of central tendency. Each one has a unique way it is calculated, and each one gives a slightly different perspective on the data set. Whenever you give a measure of central tendency, always make sure the units are the same. If the data has different units, such as hours, minutes, and seconds, convert all the data to the same unit, and use the same unit in the measure of central tendency. If no units are given in the data, do not give units for the measure of central tendency.

Mean

The **statistical mean** of a group of data is the same as the arithmetic average of that group. To find the mean of a set of data, first convert each value to the same units, if necessary. Then find the sum of all the values, and count the total number of data values, making sure you take into consideration each individual value. If a value appears more than once, count it more than once. Divide the sum of the values by the total number of values and apply the units, if any. Note that the mean does not have to be one of the data values in the set, and may not divide evenly.

$$\text{mean} = \frac{\text{sum of the data values}}{\text{quantity of data values}}$$

The mean of the data set {88, 72, 61, 90, 97, 68, 88, 79, 86, 93, 97, 71, 80, 84, 89, 72, 91, 95, 89, 83, 94, 90, 63, 69, 89} would be the sum of the twenty-five numbers divided by 25:

$$\frac{88 + 72 + 61 + 90 + 97 + \cdots + 94 + 90 + 63 + 69 + 89}{25}$$

$$= \frac{2078}{25}$$

$$= 83.12$$

While the mean is relatively easy to calculate and averages are understood by most people, the mean can be very misleading if used as the sole measure of central tendency. If the data set has outliers (data values that are unusually high or unusually low compared to the rest of the data values), the mean can be very distorted, especially if the data set has a small number of values. If unusually high values are countered with unusually low values, the mean is not affected as much. For example, if five of twenty students in a class get a 100 on a test, but the other 15 students have

- 35 -

an average of 60 on the same test, the class average would appear as 70. Whenever the mean is skewed by outliers, it is always a good idea to include the median as an alternate measure of central tendency.

Median

The **statistical median** is the value in the middle of the set of data. To find the median, list all data values in order from smallest to largest or from largest to smallest. Any value that is repeated in the set must be listed the number of times it appears. If there are an odd number of data values, the median is the value in the middle of the list. If there is an even number of data values, the median is the arithmetic mean of the two middle values.

Mode

The **statistical mode** is the data value that occurs the most number of times in the data set. It is possible to have exactly one mode, more than one mode, or no mode. To find the mode of a set of data, arrange the data like you do to find the median (all values in order, listing all multiples of data values). Count the number of times each value appears in the data set. If all values appear an equal number of times, there is no mode. If one value appears more than any other value, that value is the mode. If two or more values appear the same number of times, but there are other values that appear fewer times and no values that appear more times, all of those values are the modes.

The big disadvantage of using the median as a measure of central tendency is that is relies solely on a value's relative size as compared to the other values in the set. When the individual values in a set of data are evenly dispersed, the median can be an accurate tool. However, if there is a group of rather large values or a group of rather small values that are not offset by a different group of values, the information that can be inferred from the median may not be accurate because the distribution of values is skewed.

The main disadvantage of the mode is that the values of the other data in the set have no bearing on the mode. The mode may be the largest value, the smallest value, or a value anywhere in between in the set. The mode only tells which value or values, if any, occurred the most number of times. It does not give any suggestions about the remaining values in the set.

Dispersion

The **measure of dispersion** is a single value that helps to "interpret" the measure of central tendency by providing more information about how the data values in the set are distributed about the measure of central tendency. The measure of dispersion helps to eliminate or reduce the disadvantages of using the mean, median, or mode as a single measure of central tendency, and give a more accurate picture of the dataset as a whole. To have a measure of dispersion, you must know or calculate the range, standard deviation, or variance of the data set.

Range

The **range** of a set of data is the difference between the greatest and lowest values of the data in the set. To calculate the range, you must first make sure the units for all data values are the same, and then identify the greatest and lowest values. Use the formula $range = highest\ value - lowest\ value$. If there are multiple data values that are equal for the highest or lowest, just use one of the values in the formula. Write the answer with the same units as the data values you used to do the calculations.

Standard Deviation

Standard deviation is a measure of dispersion that compares all the data values in the set to the mean of the set to give a more accurate picture. To find the standard deviation of a population, use the formula

$$\sigma = \sqrt{\frac{\sum_{i=1}^{n}(x_i - \bar{x})^2}{n}}$$

where σ is the standard deviation of a population, x represents the individual values in the data set, $\bar{x}$ is the mean of the data values in the set, and n is the number of data values in the set. The higher the value of the standard deviation is, the greater the variance of the data values from the mean. The units associated with the standard deviation are the same as the units of the data values.

Variance

The **variance** of a population, or just variance, is the square of the standard deviation of that population. While the mean of a set of data gives the average of the set and gives information about where a specific data value lies in relation to the average, the variance of the population gives information about the degree to which the data values are spread out and tell you how close an individual value is to the average compared to the other values. The units associated with variance are the same as the units of the data values squared.

Percentile

Percentiles and **quartiles** are other methods of describing data within a set. *Percentiles* tell what percentage of the data in the set fall below a specific point. For example, achievement test scores are often given in percentiles. A score at the 80th percentile is one which is equal to or higher than 80 percent of the scores in the set. In other words, 80 percent of the scores were lower than that score.

Quartile

Quartiles are percentile groups that make up quarter sections of the data set. The first quartile is the 25th percentile. The second quartile is the 50th percentile; this is also the median of the dataset. The third quartile is the 75th percentile.

Skewness

Skewness is a way to describe the symmetry or asymmetry of the distribution of values in a dataset. If the distribution of values is symmetrical, there is no skew. In general the closer the mean of a data set is to the median of the data set, the less skew there is. Generally, if the mean is to the right of the median, the data set is *positively skewed*, or right-skewed, and if the mean is to the left of the median, the data set is *negatively skewed*, or left-skewed. However, this rule of thumb is not infallible. When the data values are graphed on a curve, a set with no skew will be a perfect bell curve. To estimate skew, use the formula

$$\text{skew} = \frac{\sqrt{n(n-1)}}{n-2}\left(\frac{\frac{1}{n}\sum_{i=1}^{n}(x_i - \bar{x})^3}{\left(\frac{1}{n}\sum_{i=1}^{n}(x_i - \bar{x})^2\right)^{\frac{3}{2}}}\right)$$

where n is the number of values is the set, x_i is the ith value in the set, and $\bar{x}$ is the mean of the set.

Simple Regression

In statistics, **simple regression** is using an equation to represent a relation between an independent and dependent variables. The independent variable is also referred to as the explanatory variable or the predictor, and is generally represented by the variable x in the equation. The dependent variable, usually represented by the variable y, is also referred to as the response variable. The equation may be any type of function – linear, quadratic, exponential, etc. The best way to handle this task is to use the regression feature of your graphing calculator. This will easily give you the curve of best fit and provide you with the coefficients and other information you need to derive an equation.

Line of Best Fit

In a scatter plot, the **line of best fit** is the line that best shows the trends of the data. The line of best fit is given by the equation $\hat{y} = ax + b$, where a and b are the regression coefficients. The regression coefficient a is also the slope of the line of best fit, and b is also the y-coordinate of the point at which the line of best fit crosses the x-axis. Not every point on the scatter plot will be on the line of best fit. The differences between the y-values of the points in the scatter plot and the corresponding y-values according to the equation of the line of best fit are the residuals. The line of best fit is also called the least-squares regression line because it is also the line that has the lowest sum of the squares of the residuals.

Correlation Coefficient

The **correlation coefficient** is the numerical value that indicates how strong the relationship is between the two variables of a linear regression equation. A correlation coefficient of –1 is a perfect negative correlation. A correlation coefficient of +1 is a perfect positive correlation. Correlation coefficients close to –1 or +1 are very strong correlations. A correlation coefficient equal to zero indicates there is no correlation between the two variables. This test is a good indicator of whether or not the equation for the line of best fit is accurate. The formula for the correlation coefficient is

$$r = \frac{\sum_{i=1}^{n}(x_i - \bar{x})(y_i - \bar{y})}{\sqrt{\sum_{i=1}^{n}(x_i - \bar{x})^2}\sqrt{\sum_{i=1}^{n}(y_i - \bar{y})^2}}$$

where r is the correlation coefficient, n is the number of data values in the set, (x_i, y_i) is a point in the set, and $\bar{x}$ and $\bar{y}$ are the means.

Z-Score

A **z-score** is an indication of how many standard deviations a given value falls from the mean. To calculate a z-score, use the formula $= \frac{x-\mu}{\sigma}$, where x is the data value, μ is the mean of the data set, and σ is the standard deviation of the population. If the z-score is positive, the data value lies above the mean. If the z-score is negative, the data value falls below the mean. These scores are useful in interpreting data such as standardized test scores, where every piece of data in the set has been counted, rather than just a small random sample. In cases where standard deviations are calculated from a random sample of the set, the z-scores will not be as accurate.

Central Limit Theorem

According to the *central limit theorem*, regardless of what the original distribution of a sample is, the distribution of the means tends to get closer and closer to a normal distribution as the sample size gets larger and larger (this is necessary because the sample is becoming more all-encompassing of the elements of the population). As the sample size gets larger, the distribution of the sample mean will approach a normal distribution with a mean of the population mean and a variance of the population variance divided by the sample size.

Shape of Data Distribution

Symmetry and Skewness

Symmetry is a characteristic of the shape of the plotted data. Specifically, it refers to how well the data on one side of the median *mirrors* the data on the other side.

A **skewed data** set is one that has a distinctly longer or fatter tail on one side of the peak or the other. A data set that is *skewed left* has more of its values to the left of the peak, while a set that is *skewed right* has more of its values to the right of the peak. When actually looking at the graph, these names may seem counterintuitive since, in a left-skewed data set, the bulk of the values seem to be on the right side of the graph, and vice versa. However, if the graph is viewed strictly in relation to the peak, the direction of skewness makes more sense.

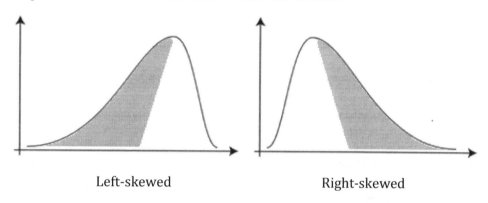

Left-skewed   Right-skewed

Unimodal vs. Bimodal

If a distribution has a single peak, it would be considered **unimodal**. If it has two discernible peaks it would be considered **bimodal**. Bimodal distributions may be an indication that the set of data being considered is actually the combination of two sets of data with significant differences.

Uniformity

A uniform distribution is a distribution in which there is *no distinct peak or variation* in the data. No values or ranges are particularly more common than any other values or ranges.

Displaying Information

Charts and Tables

Charts and tables are ways of organizing information into separate rows and columns that are labeled to identify and explain the data contained in them. Some charts and tables are organized horizontally, with row lengths giving the details about the labeled information. Other charts and tables are organized vertically, with column heights giving the details about the labeled information.

Frequency Tables

Frequency tables show how frequently each unique value appears in the set. A *relative frequency table* is one that shows the proportions of each unique value compared to the entire set. Relative frequencies are given as percents; however, the total percent for a relative frequency table will not necessarily equal 100 percent due to rounding. An example of a frequency table with relative frequencies is below.

Favorite Color	Frequency	Relative Frequency
Blue	4	13%
Red	7	22%
Purple	3	9%
Green	6	19%
Cyan	12	38%

Pictographs

A **pictograph** is a graph, generally in the horizontal orientation, that uses pictures or symbols to represent the data. Each pictograph must have a key that defines the picture or symbol and gives the quantity each picture or symbol represents. Pictures or symbols on a pictograph are not always shown as whole elements. In this case, the fraction of the picture or symbol shown represents the same fraction of the quantity a whole picture or symbol stands for. For example, a row with $3\frac{1}{2}$ ears of corn, where each ear of corn represents 100 stalks of corn in a field, would equal $3\frac{1}{2} \cdot 100 = 350$ stalks of corn in the field.

Circle Graphs

Circle graphs, also known as *pie charts*, provide a visual depiction of the relationship of each type of data compared to the whole set of data. The circle graph is divided into sections by drawing radii to create central angles whose percentage of the circle is equal to the individual data's percentage of the whole set. Each 1% of data is equal to 3.6° in the circle graph. Therefore, data represented by a 90° section of the circle graph makes up 25% of the whole. When complete, a circle graph often looks like a pie cut into uneven wedges. The pie chart below shows the data from the frequency table referenced earlier where people were asked their favorite color.

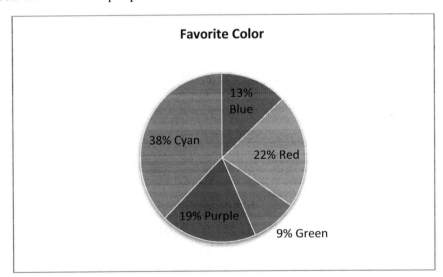

Review Video: Pie Chart
Visit mometrix.com/academy and enter code: 895285

Line Graphs

Line graphs have one or more lines of varying styles (solid or broken) to show the different values for a set of data. The individual data are represented as ordered pairs, much like on a Cartesian plane. In this case, the *x*- and *y*-axes are defined in terms of their units, such as dollars or time. The individual plotted points are joined by line segments to show whether the value of the data is increasing (line sloping upward), decreasing (line sloping downward) or staying the same (horizontal line). Multiple sets of data can be graphed on the same line graph to give an easy visual comparison. An example of this would be graphing achievement test scores for different groups of students over the same time period to see which group had the greatest increase or decrease in performance from year-to-year (as shown below).

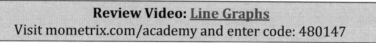

Review Video: Line Graphs
Visit mometrix.com/academy and enter code: 480147

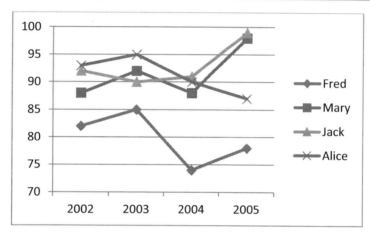

Line Plots

A **line plot**, also known as a *dot plot*, has plotted points that are not connected by line segments. In this graph, the horizontal axis lists the different possible values for the data, and the vertical axis lists the number of times the individual value occurs. A single dot is graphed for each value to show the number of times it occurs. This graph is more closely related to a bar graph than a line graph. Do not connect the dots in a line plot or it will misrepresent the data.

Review Video: Line Plot
Visit mometrix.com/academy and enter code: 754610

Stem and Leaf Plots

A **stem and leaf plot** is useful for depicting groups of data that fall into a range of values. Each piece of data is separated into two parts: the first, or left, part is called the stem; the second, or right, part is called the leaf. Each stem is listed in a column from smallest to largest. Each leaf that has the common stem is listed in that stem's row from smallest to largest. For example, in a set of two-digit numbers, the digit in the tens place is the stem, and the digit in the ones place is the leaf. With a stem and leaf plot, you can easily see which subset of numbers (10s, 20s, 30s, etc.) is the largest. This information is also readily available by looking at a histogram, but a stem and leaf plot also allows you to look closer and see exactly which values fall in that range. Using all of the test scores from above, we can assemble a stem and leaf plot like the one below.

Test Scores

7	4	8							
8	2	5	7	8	8				
9	0	0	1	2	2	3	5	8	9

Bar Graphs

A **bar graph** is one of the few graphs that can be drawn correctly in two different configurations – both horizontally and vertically. A bar graph is similar to a line plot in the way the data is organized on the graph. Both axes must have their categories defined for the graph to be useful. Rather than placing a single dot to mark the point of the data's value, a bar, or thick line, is drawn from zero to the exact value of the data, whether it is a number, percentage, or other numerical value. Longer bar lengths correspond to greater data values. To read a bar graph, read the labels for the axes to find the units being reported. Then look where the bars end in relation to the scale given on the corresponding axis and determine the associated value.

The bar chart below represents the responses from our favorite color survey.

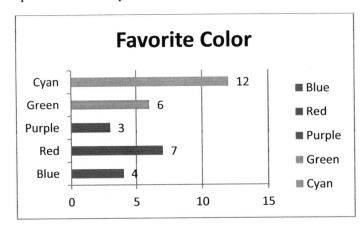

Review Video: <u>Bar Graph</u>
Visit mometrix.com/academy and enter code: 226729

Histograms

At first glance, a **histogram** looks like a vertical bar graph. The difference is that a bar graph has a separate bar for each piece of data and a histogram has one continuous bar for each *range* of data. For example, a histogram may have one bar for the range 0–9, one bar for 10–19, etc. While a bar graph has numerical values on one axis, a histogram has numerical values on both axes. Each range is of equal size, and they are ordered left to right from lowest to highest. The height of each column on a histogram represents the number of data values within that range. Like a stem and leaf plot, a histogram makes it easy to glance at the graph and quickly determine which range has the greatest quantity of values. A simple example of a histogram is below.

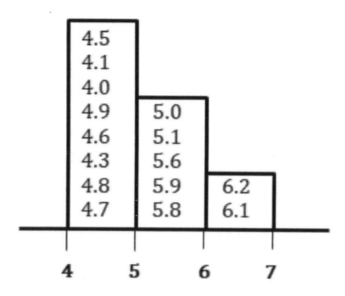

Bivariate Data

Bivariate data is simply data from two different variables. (The prefix *bi-* means *two*.) In a *scatter plot*, each value in the set of data is plotted on a grid similar to a Cartesian plane, where each axis represents one of the two variables. By looking at the pattern formed by the points on the grid, you can often determine whether or not there is a relationship between the two variables, and what that relationship is, if it exists. The variables may be directly proportionate, inversely proportionate, or show no proportion at all. It may also be possible to determine if the data is linear, and if so, to find an equation to relate the two variables. The following scatter plot shows the relationship between preference for brand "A" and the age of the consumers surveyed.

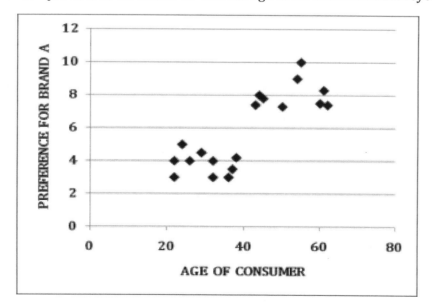

- 43 -

Scatter Plots

Scatter plots are also useful in determining the type of function represented by the data and finding the simple regression. Linear scatter plots may be positive or negative. Nonlinear scatter plots are generally exponential or quadratic. Below are some common types of scatter plots:

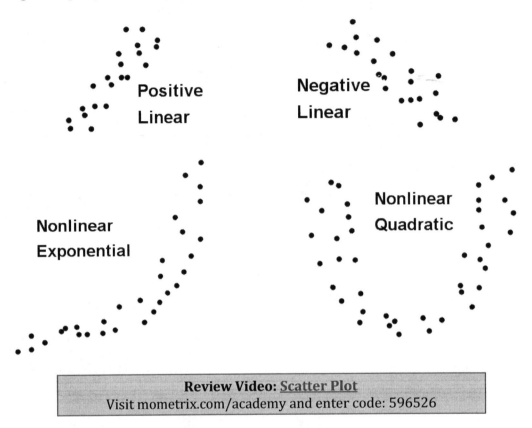

5-Number Summary

The **5-number summary** of a set of data gives a very informative picture of the set. The five numbers in the summary include the minimum value, maximum value, and the three quartiles. This information gives the reader the range and median of the set, as well as an indication of how the data is spread about the median.

Box and Whisker Plots

A **box-and-whisker plot** is a graphical representation of the 5-number summary. To draw a box-and-whiskers plot, plot the points of the 5-number summary on a number line. Draw a box whose ends are through the points for the first and third quartiles. Draw a vertical line in the box through the median to divide the box in half. Draw a line segment from the first quartile point to the minimum value, and from the third quartile point to the maximum value.

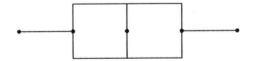

<u>68-95-99.7 Rule</u>

The **68–95–99.7 rule** describes how a normal distribution of data should appear when compared to the mean. This is also a description of a normal bell curve. According to this rule, 68 percent of the data values in a normally distributed set should fall within one standard deviation of the mean (34 percent above and 34 percent below the mean), 95 percent of the data values should fall within two standard deviations of the mean (47.5 percent above and 47.5 percent below the mean), and 99.7 percent of the data values should fall within three standard deviations of the mean, again, equally distributed on either side of the mean. This means that only 0.3 percent of all data values should fall more than three standard deviations from the mean. On the graph below, the normal curve is centered on the y-axis. The x-axis labels are how many standard deviations away from the center you are.

Therefore, it is easy to see how the 68-95-99.7 rule can apply.

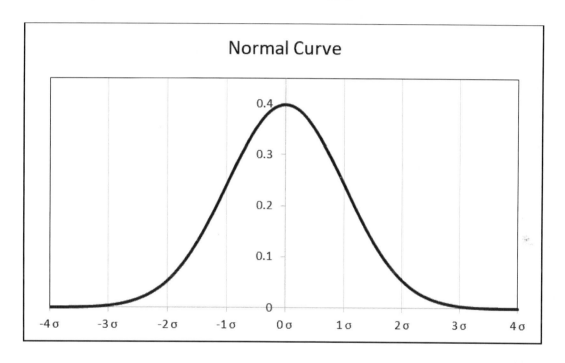

<u>Shapes of Frequency Curves</u>

The five general **shapes of frequency curves** are *symmetrical*, u-*shaped*, *skewed*, j-*shaped*, and *multimodal*. Symmetrical curves are also known as bell curves or normal curves. Values equidistant from the median have equal frequencies. U-shaped curves have two maxima – one at each end. Skewed curves have the maximum point off-center. Curves that are negative skewed, or left skewed, have the maximum on the right side of the graph so there is longer tail and lower slope on the left side. The opposite is true for curves that are positive-skewed, or right-skewed. J-shaped curves have a maximum at one end and a minimum at the other end. Multimodal curves have multiple maxima. For example, if the curve has exactly two maxima, it is called a bimodal curve.

Interpretation of Graphs

<u>Example</u>

The following graph shows the ages of five patients being cared for in a hospital:

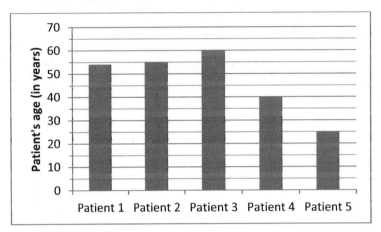

Determine the range of patient ages.

Patient 1 is 54 years old; Patient 2 is 55 years old; Patient 3 is 60 years old; Patient 4 is 40 years old; and Patient 5 is 25 years old. The range of patient ages is the age of the oldest patient minus the age of the youngest patient. In other words, $60 - 25 = 35$. The range of ages is 35 years.

Consistency between Studies

<u>Example</u>

In a drug study containing 100 patients, a new cholesterol drug was found to decrease low-density lipoprotein (LDL) levels in 25% of the patients. In a second study containing 50 patients, the same drug administered at the same dosage was found to decrease LDL levels in 50% of the patients. Are the results of these two studies **consistent** with one another?

Even though in both studies 25 people (25% of 100 is 25 and 50% of 50 is 25) showed improvements in their LDL levels, the results of the studies are inconsistent. The results of the second study indicate that the drug has a much higher efficacy (desired result) than the results of the first study. Because 50 out of 150 total patients showed improvement on the medication, one could argue that the drug is effective in one third (or approximately 33%) of patients. However, one should be wary of the reliability of results when they're not **reproducible** from one study to the next and when the **sample size** is fairly low.

Classroom Instruction

Evaluating student writing

The evaluation of student writing should be structured to include three basic goals:

1. To provide students a description of what they are doing when they respond
2. To provide a pathway for potential improvement
3. To help students learn to evaluate themselves

To fulfill these goals, it is necessary for the concept of evaluation to be broadened beyond correcting or judging students. Any teacher response to a student's response should be considered part of the evaluation. In responding to student's responses, a teacher may use written or taped comments, dialogue with students, or conferencing between teacher and students to discuss classroom performance. Students may be asked to evaluate themselves and a teacher, and students can review past progress and plan directions for potential improvement.

Components of formulating a teacher's response

There are seven basic components of a teacher's response to be considered:

1. Praise provides positive reinforcement for the student. Praise should be specific enough to bolster the student's confidence.
2. Describing provides feedback on a teacher's responses to student responses. This is best done in a conversational, non-judgmental mode.
3. Diagnosing is determining the student's unique set of strengths, attitudes, needs, and abilities. This evaluation should take into consideration all elements of the student.
4. Judging is evaluating the level, depth, insightfulness, completeness, and validity of a student's responses. This evaluation will depend on the criteria implied in the instructional approach.
5. Predicting anticipates the potential improvement of a student's responses based on specific criteria.
6. Recordkeeping is the process of recording a student's reading interests, attitudes, and use of literary strategies to chart student progress across time. Both qualitative and quantitative assessments may be used.
7. Recognition acknowledges a student's growth and progress.

Literary tests and assessments

Literary tests are measures of a student's individual performance. Literary assessments are measures of performance of a group of students without reference to individuals. Tests take into consideration what the teacher has taught the students, whereas assessments do not.

For either tests or assessments, the teacher needs a clear purpose on which to base questions or activities. Students should be told of the purpose of the tests or assessments so they will know what to expect. Tests should be used sparingly as one tool among many that can be used to evaluate students. Tests should encourage students on formulation of responses rather than rote answers. They should evaluate students on the basis of their responses rather than correct answers. Improvement over time may be noted and the students praised for specific responses.

Standardized achievement tests

These multiple-choice tests measure students' ability to understand text passages or apply literary concepts to texts. Although these tests are widely used, they have many limitations. They tend to be based on a simplistic model that ignores the complex nature of a reader's engagement with a text. These tests also do not measure students' articulation of responses. The purpose of these tests is to rank students in group norms so that half the students are below the norm.

To accurately measure a student's abilities, teachers should employ open-ended written or oral-response activities. In developing such tests, teachers must know what specific response patterns they wish to measure. The steps involved in measuring these response patterns must be clearly outlined. Teachers may wish to design questions that encourage personal expressions of responses. This would obviate the pitfall of testing primarily facts about literature rather than how students relate and use this information to engage texts.

Assessing attitudes toward literature

An important element in teaching literature is to understand the attitudes of students about reading and studying text. This may be done by group or individual interviews encouraging students to discuss their feelings about literature. Another way to measure attitudes is with a paper-and-pencil rating scale using six- or eight-point Liker scales. This type of assessment can be refined to explore preferences in form and genre.

Another type of assessment is done by using semantic scales to indicate students' interest (or lack thereof) in reading in general and favored forms and genres.

Questionnaires can be developed to learn more about students' habits regarding literature. Typical questions could be: Do you use the library regularly? Do you read books or periodicals? What types of reading do you do? Comparisons before and after instruction can indicate the effect of the instruction on habits and attitudes about literature.

Classroom-based research

Teachers can conduct their own informal descriptive research to assess the effects of their teaching on students' responses. This allows teachers an opportunity to review and reflect on their instructional methods and results. This research can take many forms, including the following:

- An analysis of students' perceptions of guided response activities to determine which were most effective
- An analysis of students' small- and large-group discussions
- A teacher self-analysis of taped, written, or conference feedback to students' writing
- Interviews with students about their responses and background experiences and attitudes
- Evaluating students' responses to texts commonly used in their instruction

These are only a few possibilities for effective classroom-based research. Any research that provides insight into student needs and preferences can be a valuable tool.

Conducting classroom research

Teachers must always keep in mind the purposes driving the research. Evaluation itself is relatively easy; the challenge is using the evaluations to help both students and teachers to grow and become better at what they are doing.

- Create a research question related to literature instruction or responses.
- Summarize the theory and research related to the topic.
- Describe the participants, setting, tasks, and methods of analysis.
- Summarize the results of the research in a graph, table, or report.
- Interpret or give reasons for the results.
- Draw conclusions from the results that suggest ways to improve instruction and evaluation of students.

Assessing instructional methods

Assessing instructional methods within a school, district, or state can help determine instructional goals and techniques relative to overall system goals. Results can indicate needed changes in the curriculum and can help an accreditation process measure the quality of an English or literature program.

An effective assessment usually includes interviews, questionnaires, and classroom observation. Trained observers rate the general type of instruction being provided (e.g., lectures, modeling and small groups), the focus of instruction (e.g., novels, poetry, drama et cetera), the critical approach used, the response strategies used and the response activities employed. Observers may also analyze the statements of goals and objectives in a curriculum, as well as the scope and sequence of the curriculum. Additionally, interviews of both students and teachers are helpful in getting firsthand accounts of instruction and results.

Building and supporting of arguments

A curriculum that is project-based begins with explicit questions meant to stimulate the curiosity of students and serve as a basis for launching various research ideas and directions. Teachers can see that curricular units provide a valuable advantage in motivating students with regard to developing hypotheses, finding research information in many sources of data in order to confirm or argue the hypotheses, and in developing arguments which are based upon understanding certain intended concepts. The Internet can provide a wealth of information but can also provide challenges for teachers. Students with literacy challenges have difficulties finding information, identifying relevant information and then reading that which they find. These challenges may at times be linked to the inability of a student to draw conceptual parallels in content and then translate them into an Internet search.

Culturally-relevant approaches

Teachers should develop learning environments that are reflective of their students' social, cultural and linguistic experiences. These serve as instructors, mediators, guides, consultants and advocates for students in helping them to find a way that is most effective to connect their cultural and community-based knowledge to their learning experiences in the classroom. A key criterion for teaching that is culturally relevant is nurturing and supporting competence in cultures both at school and at home. Teachers should use the student's home cultural experience as a base on which

- 49 -

to build skills and increase knowledge. Content that is learned in this manner becomes more significant to the student and helps facilitate a transfer of school learning to real-life.

Summative assessment

Summative assessment is carried out less frequently by the teacher; it is appropriate for checking knowledge at the end of a unit of study or at the end of the course. Whereas formative assessment is an assessment *for* learning, in that it helps the teacher to make positive adjustments to the course, summative assessment is an assessment *of* learning. It is likely that the means of summative assessment will be affected by the performance of students on formative assessments. It is important that summative assessments provide a comprehensive evaluation of students' mastery of the material, such that every area of knowledge is questioned and every skill is tested. Also, summative assessment should include questions of varying difficulty, so that students can distinguish themselves.

Charismatic authority

Max Weber defined charismatic authority as legitimate power that an individual earns by his or her personal merit. There is no set of objective values for measuring charisma, and each society may have a different standard by which charismatic authority is assigned. A leader may combine charismatic authority with traditional or legal authority, as for instance in the case of John F. Kennedy. Other recent charismatic leaders include Cesar Chavez, Martin Luther King, and Mahatma Gandhi. Charismatic authority may be wielded in subcultures and cults, as in the cases of David Koresh or Charles Manson, and, unlike the other forms of authority, it may easily disappear.

Literacy differing across content areas

Studies have shown that it is impossible to separate practices in the classroom such as strategies for activating prior knowledge from the larger cultural and social contexts in which the practices exist. Researchers say that a need exists for adolescent literacy that includes the adolescent's literacy practices beyond the confines of the classroom setting, their expanded conceptions of text such as the Internet, and the relationship that exists between the development of identity and literacy. However, the need for additional research in the teaching and learning of context in secondary schools still exists. For instance, more study is needed on the interactions between student and teacher, and between student and student; also on how students perceive themselves as readers, what their interests are at a particular time, and how institutional configurations affect the daily events occurring both in and out of school.

Reading disorder

Students who have a reading disorder have problems with their reading skills. Their skills are significantly below that which is normal for the student's age, intelligence, and education. The poor reading skills can cause problems with the student's academic success and in other areas of life. Signs associated with reading disorders include poor word recognition in reading, very slow reading, or making many mistakes. They may also show poor comprehension. Students who suffer from reading disorders normally have low self-esteem, social problems, and a higher drop-out rate in school. Reading disorders may be associated with conduct disorder, attention deficit disorder, depression, or other learning disorders. Reading disorders are usually brought to the attention of a child's parents in kindergarten or the first grade, when reading instruction becomes a very important facet of teaching.

Selecting tests

When selecting tests, care should be taken to ensure the test is not biased or offensive with regard to race, sex, native language, geographic region, or ethnic origin, as well as other factors. Those who develop tests are expected to show sensitivity to the test-takers' demographic. Steps can be taken during test development and documentation to minimize the influence of cultural factors on the test scores. These may include evaluating the items for offensiveness and cultural dependency, and using statistics to identify differential item difficulty. Questions to ask include: "Were the tests analyzed statistically for bias?" "What method was used?" "How were the items selected for the final version?" "Should the test be used with non-native English speakers?"

Social class and family background variables in emergent literacy

The social class and family background variables are prominent in emergent literacy research. Numerous studies have addressed links between parental occupation, income, and children's achievements. One finding is that there are wide variations in children's achievements, regardless of social class in relation to a child's early literacy experiences. Specific factors in family environments such as parental interest, positive attitudes, and modeling have been identified as major predictors of academic success despite social class or educational levels. There is considerable variation among family environments in the status and value given to books, the presence of materials for writing, and the time that is spent reading and writing. Studies have shown that early readers tend to come from homes with more pencils, paper, and books, and that have mothers who read more often.

Social learning and mediation

Along with genetic analysis, social learning and mediation are the three major components of a sociocultural approach to literacy. Social learning refers to the social origin of mental functioning. Vygotsky said that every function in the child's cultural development appears first on the social level and later on the individual level. The first development is between people and the second is inside the child. Vygotsky also believed the development occurred through such means as apprenticeship learning, or interaction with teachers and peers. This view looks at learning not as an isolated act of cognition but rather a process of gaining entry to a discourse of practitioners. Mediation is the notion that all human activity is mediated through signs or tools. It is not so much the tools, such as computers or writing, by themselves as it is how they transform human action in a fundamental way.

Multiliteracies

A great deal of interest has risen around the world in the future of literacy teaching through so-called "multiliteracies." The multiliteracies argument is that our personal, public, and working lives are currently changing in some very significant ways and that these changes have the effect of transforming cultures and the ways in which we communicate. The ramification of this is that the way literacy is now taught will become obsolete and what counts for literacy must also change. Multiliteracies has at its heart two major and closely related changes. First is the growing significance of cultural and linguistic diversity. This is reinforced every day by modern media. Each day, both globally and in our local communities, we have to negotiate differences that are interconnected with our working and community lives. As this happens, English is becoming a world language. The second major shift is the influence of new communications technologies.

Literacy starting at home

Children's school readiness is influenced by their parents' educational levels. The higher the parents' education, the more likely the child will succeed in school. Children who are raised in literate homes are likely to enter first grade with several thousand hours of 1-to-1 pre-reading experience. Children have a better chance of becoming fully literate adults if they are encouraged to read at home. Studies have shown that improving parents' skills positively affects their children's language development. Without parental support, the cycle of under-education will continue in families from generation to generation. With support from family literacy programs, children who may have otherwise been educationally and developmentally behind their peers came into school on par with their peers.

Phonemic awareness

Different levels of phonemic awareness in terms of abilities include:

- Hearing rhymes and alliteration as measured by knowing nursery rhymes.
- Doing tasks such as comparing and contrasting the sounds of words for rhyme and alliteration, also known as oddity tasks.
- Blending and splitting syllables.
- Performing phonemic segmenting such as counting out the number of phonemes contained in a word.
- Performing tasks of phoneme manipulation such as adding or deleting a particular phoneme.

Instruction in phonemic awareness might include:

- Engaging preschool children in activities that direct their attention to sounds in words, such as rhyming games.
- Teaching segmentation and blending.
- Combining letter-sound relationship instruction with segmentation and blending.
- Sequencing examples systematically when teaching blending and segmentation.

Children of kindergarten age require development of phonemic awareness by hearing, identifying, and manipulating phonemes or individual sounds within spoken words. Once children acquire knowledge of letters, they can be taught to perform activities to isolate phonemes and achieve phoneme segmentation by pointing to or manipulating letters along with sounds. Blending and segmentation in phonemic awareness is important because they provide a foundation for skills such as spelling. Studies have shown that phonemic awareness can be acquired with as little as 20 hours of instruction, although some children might require more instruction in order to accurately segment words. The individual students should be assessed to verify that the instruction was successful. More instruction might be required for some children than others.

Phonemic awareness is difficult because:

- There are about 40 phonemes or sound units in the English language despite there being only 26 letters in the alphabet.
- There are 250 different spellings representing distinct sounds such as "f," which may be represented as "ph" or "gh."

- Phonemes, or sound units, are not necessarily obvious. They must be learned. The sounds that make up words are not distinctly separate from one other, a state referred to as being "coarticulated." Additionally, words such as "fat" and "hat" are said to have different phonemes "f" and "h" in English despite little difference in sound to distinguish the words. These are called a "minimal pair." If no minimal pair can be found to demonstrate two distinct sounds, these sounds may be termed "allophones," which are variant sounds not recognized by a speaker as distinct and as such are not significantly different in language. They are therefore looked upon as being the same.

Sing-songs

Rhyme is a prominent feature of many songs. Listening to and singing songs helps make children aware of the phonemic nature of spoken language. Songs that help children to manipulate sounds in words are most effective in having children pay attention to a language's sound structure. Manipulating sounds in words can be challenging for those children in the early stages of phonemic awareness development, so children should be given many opportunities to learn the songs before they start trying to manipulate the sounds. One way this can be done is to play tapes of such songs during transitional activities such as snack time or clean-up time in order to help children become more familiar with sound play.

Social constructivism

Social constructivism is a variant of cognitive constructivism that puts an emphasis on the collaborative nature of learning. This theory was developed by Soviet psychologist Lev Vygotsky. He was a cognitivist but he rejected postulations by other cognitivists such as Piaget and Perry which said that separating learning from its social context was possible. Vygotsky theorized that all cognitive functions originate and must be explained as products of social interactions and that learning was not simply the accommodation and assimilation of new knowledge attained by those learning. Instead, he felt it was the process by which learners were integrated into a community of knowledge. Vygotsky believed that the cultural development of children appears first on the social level and only later inside the child. This applies equally in voluntary attention to logical memories and forming concepts. Higher functions come from actual relationships between people, Vygotsky postulated.

Stages of reading for young children

Children gain literacy through emergent, beginning, and fluent stages. The emergent stage is marked by children noticing environmental print, showing interest in books, pretending to read, and using picture cues and predictable patterns in books in order to retell a story. They also can identify some letters, reread books with patterns that are predictable, and recognize up to 10 familiar words. The beginning stage will show the child identifying letter names and sounds; matching written and spoken words; using the beginning, middle, and ending sounds to decode words; recognizing as many as 100 high-frequency words; reading slowly, word by word; and self-correcting while they are reading. The fluent stage features automatic identification with most words, reading with expression, reading at about 100 words per minute or more, preferring to read silently, recognizing up to 300 high-frequency words, and often reading independently making inferences.

Reading proficiency at a young age

There is strong evidence that young people who are not fluent readers and writers by the end of the third grade may never catch up with their peers. One study found that first graders who were not on grade level by the end of the year stood a 1-in-10 chance of never having proficiency at grade level in reading. A governor of Indiana indicated that the determination of how many new prison beds to build was based, in part, on the number of second graders who do not read at second grade level. The number of future prison beds in California depends on numbers of children who do not go past the fourth grade reading level.

Lexical affixes

Lexical affixes, also known as semantic affixes, are bound elements that appear as affixes, but function as incorporated nouns within verbs and as elements of compound nouns. In other words, they are similar to word roots or stems in function, but are similar to affixes in form. Although they are similar to incorporated nouns, lexical affixes differ in that they never occur in freestanding nouns. They always appear as affixes. Such affixes are relatively rare. Lexical suffixes often bear little or no resemblance to free nouns with similar meaning. When used, lexical suffixes usually have more general meanings. For instance, a language may have a lexical suffix that means water in a general sense, but not have a noun equivalent referring to water in general. Instead it may have several nouns with more specific meanings, such as saltwater or groundwater.

Form function of oral language

The form function of oral language consists of phonology, morphology, and syntax. Phonology is the system of phonemes or sounds in language. Morphology is the system of rules governing word structure and organization. Many sounds have no meaning by themselves; these are phonemes. Every morpheme, however, has meaning on its own, as a root word, or attached to a root word as a prefix, suffix, or word ending. In English, the normal sentence is structured as subject + verb + object. Syntax refers to the way in which words are combined into sentences. Students with an understanding of syntax can comprehend how the various parts of a sentence relate to one another other.

Writing and cooperative writing

Specific instruction in writing for different reasons and audiences as well as instruction in strategies to help clarify and enrich language expression is crucial. Language mechanical skills such as usage, capitalization, and grammar can be taught and integrated into the students' own writing through the process of editing. For instance, students might study the use of adjectives and adverbs, and then write descriptive compositions. Cooperative learning can be a very effective upper elementary reading and writing instruction if used properly. Students should generally work in groups of four or five members that stay together for six-to-eight weeks. Each group might be presented a lesson on main idea and the students can work in groups to practice such a skill.

Word identification

The identification or recognition of words is the ability of students to develop an automaticity when reading isolated words. Automaticity refers to the speed and accuracy with which students are able to read these isolated words. Automatic words recognition is an important part of literacy because the level of students' abilities to recognize known words and decode or determine unfamiliar words can affect how fluently the students may read, and fluency is essential for comprehension. It should be remembered that building meaning is the goal of any literacy endeavor. Developing strong word recognition skills is also critical for students who, for whatever reason, did not develop strong phonological awareness in early childhood. These students may need to rely more heavily on their vocabularies and less on decoding skills.

Newspapers

Students learn when they are motivated and the topics they study hold interest and relevance to their lives. Many classrooms are using newspapers as a source for motivational and timely resources. It is a concept that dates back to 1795 when the Portland Eastern Herald in Maine published an editorial that put forth the role that newspapers can play in helping to deliver, extend, and enrich the curriculum. Classrooms around the world are using newspapers to complement text books and other relevant resources for a variety of disciplines. Newspapers featuring articles, editorials, and advertising help students apply literacy and numeracy skills as well as appreciate the importance of studying history and current affairs. Studies have shown that students who use newspapers score higher on reading comprehension tests and develop stronger critical thinking skills.

First grade reading comprehension

The process of learning to read is not a linear one. Students need not learn decoding before they learn to comprehend. Both skills should be taught at the same time, beginning at the earliest stages of instruction for reading. Comprehension strategies can be taught using both material that is read to children and material that they read for themselves. Before reading, teachers can delineate the reason for the reading: reviewing vocabulary, encouraging children to predict what stories are about, or activating background knowledge. Teachers can direct children's attention to subtle or difficult portions of the text during reading, point out difficult words and ideas and ask children to find problems and solutions. After reading, children can be taught particular metacognitive strategies such as asking themselves regularly whether what is being read makes sense.

Reciprocal teaching

In many ways, reciprocal teaching is the aggregation of four separate comprehension strategies: summarizing, questioning, clarifying, and predicting. Summarizing presents the ability to identify and integrate the information that is most important in a text. Text can be summarized across sentences and paragraphs, and also across passages. When students start the reciprocal teaching procedures they are usually focused on sentences and paragraphs. Questioning reinforces the strategy of summarizing. When students identify questions, they identify a kind of information that is important enough to provide substance for a question, then post the information in question form. Clarifying is important for students with comprehension difficulty. They are taught to be alert to the effects of comprehension impediments and to take the necessary measures to restore meaning. Predicting is when students predict what the author will discuss next in the text.

What is most important in reading education is turning out readers who can understand the meaning in texts. Reciprocal teaching is a scaffolded discussion technique for instilling some of the methods that good readers can use to comprehend text through questioning, clarifying, summarizing, and predicting. Teaching students the four strategies gives them the tools that great readers use in meeting their text-reading goals. Thus, it is the four strategies that are taught rather than reading skills. These multiple strategies help students to read by giving them a choice of strategies to be used in reading. The scaffolding gives support to help the students connect what they know and can do with what they need to do in order to be successful at learning a particular lesson. This also gives the students a chance to support each other and foster a sense of community among classmates.

The word "reciprocal" in reciprocal teaching is somewhat misleading in that it does not entail students doing the teaching. But the students use a set of four strategies—summarizing, clarifying, predicting, and questioning—to improve reading comprehension. That improvement is the ultimate goal. Other aspects of the method include:

- The teacher scaffolds instruction of the strategy by guiding, modeling, and applying the strategies.
- It guides students to become metacognitive and reflective in the use of strategies.
- It helps students monitor their comprehension of reading.
- It uses the social nature of learning in order to improve and scaffold the comprehension of reading.
- The instruction is presented through different classroom settings including whole group, guided reading groups, and literature circles.

Student note-taking

Reading for certain information and then taking notes are perhaps the most challenging steps in the process of solving information problems. Students in grades 3-8 require many developmentally-appropriate chances to locate information before the techniques are mastered. Note-taking consists of identifying keywords and related words, skimming and scanning, and extracting needed information. These steps begin after students define and narrow the task, construct researchable questions, and find the right sources. After students build researchable questions from the information needed to finish a task or solve an information problem, the questions can be transferred to graphic organizers or data charts. This can allow them to focus on the key words. Skimming and scanning will help them make use of the text with less time and effort. Information may be extracted and recorded with different forms of note-taking, including citation, summary, quotation, and paraphrasing.

Test-taking strategies

A reason for test anxiety and poor performance on tests is often a lack of preparation. Children often know about a test in advance. Some teachers also tell parents when tests will be given. Knowing when the test is scheduled and what will be covered can help give the child a study schedule to prepare for the test. One schedule is for the student to study nightly for several nights before the test. Teachers may encourage parents to determine how long the child can be expected to concentrate at a given sitting. The parent should also be encouraged by the teacher to ask the child what material might be on the test and to go over questions at the end of chapters and sections. Maps, charts, and diagrams should receive special attention. A sample test can be developed from this information, which can even make studying fun.

Students should follow directions carefully. Have the student listen and read the directions to the test so they understand what is expected of them. Teachers need to make sure the students understand vocabulary words and concepts in the directions. Words appearing in the test directions that are common should be introduced to students as part of the process of test preparation. Ensure that the students understand what they are to do. If students have questions, they should be encouraged to ask the teacher before the test starts. Listening and reading activities that will provide practice for following directions can be incorporated into the classroom. Students must know how to budget their time for the test. They should work fast but comfortably. Students can practice this.

Before the test strategy

Before a test students should:

- Begin to study the material a few days before the test and take study breaks every 20-30 minutes.
- Take time to do some kind of physical activity that will help reduce tension and stress.
- Eat a good breakfast the morning of the test and get a good night's sleep the night before the test.
- Skim the material and determine which parts are best understood and which ones are still difficult.
- Read a sentence or two and reread what they don't understand.
- Pick out main ideas or key terms and think up possible test questions by themselves.
- Read aloud and study with a partner or parent. While reading, the students should listen to themselves.
- Think about what important points the teacher talked about during class.
- Remain motivated and positive.

Emphasis on literacy in content areas

Attention should be paid to literacy in content areas for several reasons. The 2003 National Assessment of Educational Progress Reading Report shows that general test scores have improved over recent years, but very few young people in the United States can read at proficient or advanced levels. Most can decode and answer simple comprehension questions, but few can synthesize ideas, interpret the information they receive, or critique the ideas they read about, especially when they work with expository texts. Also, literacy in content areas has consequences that go beyond the ability to understand a subject-matter text. Advanced or specialized literacy forms are tools that signify success, both academically and socially, and can be important for economic, social, and political success beyond school.

Cubing

Cubing is a literacy strategy in which students are able to explore topics from six separate dimensions or viewpoints. The student can:

1. Provide a description of the particular topic.
2. Compare the topic to a different topic.
3. Associate the topic with something else and provide specific reasons for the choice.
4. Analyze the topic and tell how the topic came about.
5. Give an explanation of what the topic comprises after analysis.
6. Provide an argument for or against the topic.

The teacher chooses a topic related to the thematic unit and students are divided into six groups. Students brainstorm about their dimension ideas and then use a quick write or quick draw. These are shared with the class and are attached to the sides of a cube box. This strategy can be applicable to subjects such as social studies.

Multimedia literacy

Multimedia literacy is an aspect of literacy that is being recognized as technology expands how people communicate with each other. Literacy, as a concept, emerged as a measure of how one can read or write. It means today that someone reads or writes at a level that is adequate to communicate. Multimedia calls for a more fundamental meaning of literacy when looked upon at a societal level. Multimedia is the use of several different media to send or receive information. These include text, audio, graphics, animation, virtual reality, computer programming, and robotics. The basic literacy of reading and writing is often handled by computer these days and provides a foundation for more advanced levels of multimedia literacy.

Film and television as teaching tools

Television and film can help students explore cultural context and are easily integrated into the curriculum. They are entertaining media and allow for a great deal of flexibility in techniques of teaching and material. Surveys indicate that more teachers than ever are integrating television and videotapes into their curricula. Teachers are seeking quality programming with the appropriate structure and length, as well as advance information that allows them to preview the programming. Also found in the surveys was that both teachers and students are becoming more media savvy as they use camcorders and other video production equipment with increased frequency. That effect is likely to grow even further with such mobile video platforms as digital cameras and cell phones.

Electronic textbooks

Technology is commonly used in learning situations, such as elementary science students watching a video of an experiment being performed, middle school students manipulating commercial software that helps them prepare for a rapidly-changing technological workplace, and high school students playing interactive chemistry games on the Internet that score their manipulations of chemical equations and formulas such as those used to solve problems in real life. Technology can help a child who is blind to hear audible descriptions that allow him or her to understand procedures and participate in a particular portion of class. Students who are physically impaired can complete computer activities with commercial software that has adaptive devices to permit the student to independently complete a task. Students who are hearing impaired can use CD-ROM or Internet video with captions.

Lesson ideas that make use of technology

Various lessons can be enriched by the use of technology. This includes:

- Digital presentations. Students can show their learning in a digital presentation. They might create a Web site or create a stand-alone presentation. Students should cite their sources of information as with any research project. They should also be taught the importance of seeking permission for copyrighted matter.
- Have students read books online. Thousands of books are available online at Web sites such as Online Books Page.
- Have Web quests. This is an activity that is good for language arts and exploration of literature. The quests list sets of questions and tasks on which students can perform Internet research.
- Word processing. Word processing programs are good for projects that would require having multiple drafts.

Content-specific lesson ideas using technology

Technology can be used in lessons for a host of content areas. Some examples include:

- Language arts. The Internet can be used to look at photos described in novels and can provide information about the social fabric of the community, helping students to learn the context.
- Mathematics. Spreadsheets can be used to calculate distance, speed, and travel time between two cities. The data can be exposed in several forms to help foster the understanding of variables.
- Science. The Internet can be used to view topographic and satellite maps to help determine an area's rock formations.
- Physical education. The Internet can be used to watch basketball techniques in slow motion to help improve shooting form.

Literacy activity in which students report the news

Students are told to be reporters and report the news for their school. They are told that they will need to report on local news, world news, national news, sports, entertainment, and weather. The reporter should visit various news websites to gather information for the stories. The stories must be accurate, informative, and interesting. The audience is the students' fifth grade class so it must be in language they can understand. The teacher functions as the editor. In this exercise, the student learns the parts of the newspaper: the headline, the lead, quotes, body, and ending. There should be pre-writing planning and collection of information. The student gets à "beat" to cover, finds a story, and writes about it.

Recursive strategies for composing texts

The framework for composing texts includes invention, drafting, revision, and editing. Many recursive strategies lie inside these components. Invention refers to the ways in which a writer might think about what he or she wants to do and how it could be done. It involves using outlines, seeking other opinions and perspectives, and research. It is recursive in that writers invent throughout the act of writing, planning, revising, and editing. Drafting refers to the different versions of a text before closure. Writers discover as a result of writing a draft, and then draft some more. Some view revision as a way to see the text from different perspectives. Revision is also rethinking ideas and how they may be conveyed. Editing refers to decisions that writers make to produce writing in which the words and punctuation are correct, along with flowing sentence structure and diction.

Assignments that are personal

Assignments that make learning personal are often very effective in helping students appreciate studying and completing those assignments. Such work often lets students look into their family, community, and cultural experiences and gain a better appreciation of both their own and their peers' backgrounds. Family tree projects in social studies classes are an example because of the great diversity of most American schools. These projects or others such as historical ones in which family members are sought out may often bring out values that the students might not otherwise appreciate and can also foster closer family relationships. Making assignments personal and valuable gives students a great incentive to appreciate studying about a subject and to find learning as a quest.

Working with recent immigrant students

American schools have been a major agent for helping those children and youth who recently arrived in this country with adapting to the civic and social demands of their new homes. Classroom lessons and socialization on the school yard take place. But sometimes the home culture teachings and expectations are contrasted with those of American schools. This can lead to labeling children as disabled when no disability actually exists. These students do have issues with psychosocial stress as they attempt to adapt. A transition that is successful to one's new country requires a secure cross-cultural identity. How much of each culture forms this identity depends on the person's needs, skills, experience, education, and support. Recognition of these transitioning needs and support are among the strategic help that can be given to these children.

Students may display behaviors in their cultures that are different from those in the American mainstream; thus, they are at risk for being labeled by uninformed educators as having behaviors that are "wrong." Teachers should familiarize themselves with a student's home culture's values and practices. There should be an awareness of differences that promotes understanding, tolerance, acceptance, and celebration of others and their ways. Information on other cultures can be found in many textbooks and travel books, and on various Web sites. Another way to develop familiarity with a student's cultural background is the use of a "cultural informant." This is someone who might be familiar with the group and their ways, such as teachers or other successful members of that cultural group.

Culture capsule

A culture capsule is a biliteracy activity that is usually prepared outside class by students, but presented during class for about five or 10 minutes. It consists of a paragraph or two and explains one minimal difference between an American custom and that of another culture's custom. It also includes several photos and other information that is relevant. These capsules can be used in addition to role playing. Students may act out a part of another culture. Essentially the capsule is a brief description of some aspect of the target culture followed by contrasting information from the students' native language culture. These are done orally with teachers giving a brief talk on the chosen cultural point and then leading a discussion on cultures.

Teaching and learning culture

A framework for teaching and learning culture includes:

- Knowing about getting information. The nature of content and getting information. Facts about the United States and important facets of its culture.
- Learning objectives—demonstrating a mastery of information.
- Techniques and activities—cultural readings, films, videotapes, cultural artifacts, and personal anecdotes.
- Knowing how culture is traditionally taught. Are students given information and asked to show that they know it.
- Knowing how to develop behaviors—knowing about what facts you learned and acting upon them.
- Learning objectives—demonstrating ability, fluency, expertise, confidence, and ease.
- Techniques—dialogs, role playing, simulations, and field experiences.
- Knowing where communicative competence in the language occurs. Students know both what to say and how to say it in an appropriate manner.

Measuring changes in attitudes over foreign cultures

Ways to measure the change in attitudes about foreign cultures include:

- Social distance scales. This is to measure the degree to which one separates oneself socially from members of another culture. For instance: Would you marry, have as a close friend, have as an acquaintance, or work with someone from another culture?
- Semantic differential scales. This is to judge the defined culture group in terms of a number of traits that are bipolar. For instance, are people from this culture clean? Are they dirty? Are they good? Are they bad?
- Statements. This is to put a check in front of statements the student agrees with. Is the person you know envious of others? Self-indulgent? Quick to understand? Tactless?
- Self-esteem change. This is to measure self-esteem changes in the primary grades. For instance, am I happy with myself?

Developing personal relationships with newly arrived immigrants

Students need to feel welcomed and valued by their teacher. A direct verbal communication may not be feasible, but there are other methods of showing acceptance and personal warmth toward students. This will help relieve anxiety and can promote an enthusiasm to learn academics and American patterns of behavior. Smiles are a good way to reach different cultural, ethnic, and linguistic groups. Also, teachers should take time to talk with the youngsters, even through an interpreter. Having students talk about their prior life will help the teacher become more familiar with their concerns and enable the teacher to emotionally support the new students. The teacher may also answer questions about schools and what is needed to live here in America. The teacher may also discuss how he or she can help make the transition easier.

Becoming acquainted with a student's strengths and needs

An important part of planning and organizing for instruction is acquiring an understanding of the students. It is useful, early in the school year, to learn as much as possible about the students, what their interests, learning abilities, and learning styles are. As a teacher talks directly with each student, information is provided about how that student perceives himself or herself as a learner. Also useful is:

- Give oral or written diagnostic questionnaires or surveys to assess the students' current abilities, interests, and attitudes.
- Consult other personnel, student portfolios, and the students' records from previous years.
- Consider the potential for using previously successful adaptations with each student, and plan other adaptations to address the specific needs for learning.

Inventory of students' learning styles

A teacher wants to know what types of learning styles a student has as well as answers to other questions. These are the answers teachers must use to determine how instruction may be personalized for the students. This can also be surprising information for the students as well. An inventory of student learning styles can build self-esteem by helping the student to discover his or her strengths, learn about the areas in which more effort is required, and appreciate the differences among fellow students. A number of published inventories are available to help students determine their learning strengths. Inventories may also be found for free on the Internet.

Define these terms

Within-class ability grouping in classrooms	Research tends to support within-class ability grouping, grouping those with like abilities, as helping most students learn. It is generally flexible and not as stigmatizing as other groups. If such groups are considered, teachers might want only two such groups to make management of the grouping process easier.
Cooperative learning	Cooperative learning is an instructional strategy in which students are put into heterogeneous groups. It is perhaps one of the best researched innovations in recent times and can have dramatic student achievement effects when implemented properly.
Individualized instruction	Individualized instruction or one-on-one instruction is the best way to deal with individual student difference, but it is very difficult to accomplish. Computer-assisted instruction may change that.

Continuous progress with respect to class groupings

Continuous progress generally means that children remain with their classroom peers in an age cohort, despite having met or surpassed specific grade-level achievement expectations. This term is usually associated with an emphasis on the individualized curriculum, so that teaching and learning tasks are responsive to previous experience, and on the rate of progress of the child despite age. This practice is sometimes referred to as social promotion. The main reason for this practice is that there might be a stigmatizing effect on children if removed from their age cohort. Like ungraded approaches, the programs that are focused on continuous progress are not aimed at maximizing the educational benefits of children of different abilities and ages being together. Instead their goal is to let the children progress without being made to meet expectations of achievement.

Implications of different age grouping schemes

Grouping practices might seem to have slight distinctions but there are significant implications in practice. Ungraded or nongraded approaches indicate that age is not a good indicator of what children are ready to learn. It emphasizes regrouping children for class based on perceived readiness to acquire skills and knowledge instead of age. Its main goal is of homogenizing children for instruction based on achievement rather than age. Combined grade groupings and continuous progress practices do not intend to increase a sense of family within class or to encourage children to share knowledge and experience, but mixed-age grouping does take advantage of heterogeneity of experience and skills in a group of children.

Safe learning environments

Most incidents of school violence or serious disruption begin as less serious behavior that has escalated to the point of requiring attention. Many aggressive or disruptive behaviors that spiraled out of control could have been prevented by early and appropriate classroom responses. A well-documented knowledge base exists on how to prevent misbehavior escalation in the classrooms. A number of those programs that integrate those findings into classroom management packages have become available. Most rely on principles of effectively managing the classroom including:

- Multiple options that rely on various strategies and responses for maintaining an effective learning environment.
- Emphasizing the positive.
- Teaching responsibility.

- Decelerating emotional conflict.
- Consistently communicating appropriate behavior.
- Early responses that let the student know what the school and classroom rules are and that they will be enforced.

Book clubs

Activities in which school book clubs can grow together as a group include:

- Letting the group name themselves. Let them decide on a club mascot.
- Allowing each club to keep a group reading notebook or journal where they track their readings. Perhaps they might decorate the journal if they so wish.
- Allowing groups to decide upon projects that are inquiry-based. For example, a group might decide to explore something of specific interest to them and search for the information. After these steps are taken, teachers should explain the process and allow some class time so that students may discuss the activities and establish their first groups. Those students who are not interested in this voluntary activity can read on their own.

Define the following language disorders:

Stuttering	Stuttering is an interruption in the rhythm or flow of speech that is characterized by hesitations, repetitions, or prolongation of sounds, syllables, words, or phrases.
Articulation disorders	Articulation disorders are difficulties with the way sounds are formed and put together. They are usually characterized by substituting one sound for another (wabbit for rabbit), omitting a sound (han for hand), or distorting sounds.
Voice disorders	Voice disorders are characterized by pitches that are inappropriate, such as being too high, too low, never changing or breaking, excessive or inadequate volume, or vocal qualities such as harsh, hoarse, nasal, or breathy.
Aphasia	Aphasia is the loss of speech and language abilities as a result of a head injury or stroke.
Delayed language	Delayed language is characterized by a marked slowness in grammar and vocabulary development that is needed to express and understand ideas and thoughts.

Dyslexia

Dyslexia involves a brain difference that is not a defect but does make it excessively hard to learn language. A child with dyslexia will have problems from the very beginning in learning to understand speech and being understood. The child might need to describe what he or she wants, might have trouble sequencing words, or may speak words in an incorrect order. A child may have problems positioning letters when he or she enters school. Dyslexia is difficult to recognize because many of its manifestations are part of the natural maturing process of young children. When children get stuck in these stages and it lasts for an abnormally long period, parents and teachers should recognize this as a possible problem. But a dyslexic mind may have exceptional ability for singing or playing a musical instrument at an early age.

Various student assessment systems

Assessment system types include norm-referenced, criterion-referenced, and individual or alternative assessments. Criterion-referenced systems are those in which an individual's performance is compared to a certain learning objective of performance standard rather than the performance of other students. Norm-referenced systems are those in which student performance is compared to a "norm group," which may be a national sample that represents a diverse cross-section of students. These tests usually sort students and measure achievement based on some performance criterion. An individual assessment is one focusing on the individual student, such as a portfolio assessment. This is a portfolio of the student's classroom work. Alternative assessments are those requiring students to respond to a question rather than a set of responses.

Wide-Range Achievement Test

The Wide-Range Achievement Test is one of a number of standardized achievement assessments to determine a child's cognitive ability. It is designed for individuals ages 5-75. It contains scoring for reading, spelling, and math. It provides up to 30 minutes for each of the three forms. The test uses a single-level format as well as alternative forms. These alternative forms may be used individually or with one another in order to provide a more qualitative assessment of academic skills. The reading subtest includes letter naming and word pronunciation out of context. The spelling subtest asks the student to write his or her own name, and then write words as they are directed. The mathematical portion includes counting, reading problems, number symbols, and written computation.

Student reading inventory

To administer a student reading inventory certain materials would be needed such as a stop watch to time the student, a copy of all readings for both the student and the teacher, and comprehension questions for scoring purposes. Steps to be taken when administering the inventory include:

- Explain to students that this is not a test. Tell them that this inventory is really to tell how the teacher can teach them better.
- Set the timer.
- Begin the timer as the student reads the first excerpt aloud.
- Score errors on the teacher's copy.
- Stop the timer when the student stops and record the total time.
- Give the comprehension questions and record the answers.

Formative assessment

A formative assessment is a diagnostic use of assessment to provide feedback to teachers and students over the course of instruction. That is in contrast to a summative assessment, which usually happens after a period of instruction and requires making judgments about the learning that has occurred, such as with a test score or paper. Assessments in general include teacher observation, classroom instruction, or an analysis of student work, including homework and tests. Assessments are formative when the information is used to adapt teaching and learning to meet the needs of the students. When teachers know how students are progressing and where they are having difficulties, they can use this information to make needed instructional adjustments, such as reteaching, alternative instruction approaches, or offering more practice opportunities.

Informal assessment

Although there are no uniformly accepted definitions for formal and informal assessments, informal can mean techniques that are easily put into classroom routines, and learning activities to measure a student's learning outcome. Informal assessment can be used without interfering with instructional time. The results can be an indicator of the skills or subjects that interest a student, but they do not provide comparison to a broader group like standardized tests. Informal tests require clear understanding of the levels of a student's abilities. Informal assessments seek identification of a student's strengths and weaknesses without a regard to norms or grades. Such assessments may be done in structured or unstructured manners. Structured ones include checklists or observations. Unstructured assessments are those such as student work samples or journals.

Authentic assessment

Authentic assessment asks students to apply their skills and knowledge the same way that they would be used in real-world situations. It is a performance-based assessment that requires each student to exhibit his or her in-depth knowledge and understanding through a mastery demonstration. It is an assessment of authentic learning, which is the type of learning in which activities and materials are framed in real-life contexts. The underlying assumption of such an approach is that the material is meaningful to students, and thus more motivating and deeply processed. Some of the terms or concepts that are related to authentic learning include contextual learning and theme-based curriculum.

Constructed-response tests as opposed to selected-response

Constructed-response tests are a type of non-multiple choice exam that requires some type of written or oral response. Selected-response tests consist of questions to be answered from a predetermined list of answers, with formats that include multiple choice, true/false, matching, or fill in the blanks. Each type of test has its benefits. Selected-response formats allow more questions to be asked in shorter time periods. Scoring is faster and it is easy to create comparable test forms. Since selected-response tests can normally be answered quickly, more items that covers several content areas can be administered in a short period of time. They can also be machine-scorable tests that allow quicker and more objective scoring. Constructed-response tests have the potential for gathering deeper information about a student's knowledge and understanding of a content area. Constructed-response items are more time consuming and allow fewer items to be covered.

Portfolio assessments

A portfolio can be thought of as a scrapbook or photo album that records the progress and activities of the program and those who participate in it. It showcases them to interested parties both inside and outside of the program. Portfolios can be used to examine and measure progress by documenting the learning as it takes place. They extend beyond test scores to include a substantive picture of what a student is doing and experiencing. Portfolios are useful in documenting progress in higher-order goals such as applying skills and synthesizing experience beyond what standardized or norm-based tests can do. The portfolio contents are sometimes known as "evidence" or "artifacts." They can include drawings, writing, photos, video, audio tapes, computer discs, and copies of program-specific or standardized tests.

Portfolio assessment is best used for the following:

- Evaluating programs with flexible or individualized outcomes or goals.
- Allowing individuals and programs in the community to be involved in their own change and decisions to change.
- Giving information that provides a meaningful insight into behavioral change.

- Providing tools to ensure communications and accountability to a wide range of audiences. These participants, such as families or community members, may not be sophisticated in interpreting statistical data and can better appreciate more visual or experiential evidence of success being achieved.
- Assessing some of the more important and complex aspects of many constructs.

Portfolio assessment has these disadvantages:

- It can be very time-intensive for teachers to evaluate, especially if the portfolios must be done in addition to traditional grading and tests.
- Having to develop an individualized criteria may be unfamiliar or difficult at first.
- The portfolio could just be a collection of miscellaneous artifacts that does not show growth or progress if the goals and criteria are unclear.
- As is the case with other forms of qualitative data, the data that is used from portfolio assessments can be difficult to analyze or to aggregate in order to see progress or change in the individual student.

Portfolios used for assessment have certain essential characteristics including:

- Having multiple data sources including both people and artifacts. People can be teachers, participants, or community members. Artifacts can be test scores, drawings, writings, videotapes, or audiotapes.
- Having authentic evidence that is related to program activities.
- Being dynamic and capturing change and growth. Portfolios should include different stages of mastery which will allow a much deeper understanding of the change process.
- Being explicit in that participants should know what is expected of them.
- Being integrated, meaning having the evidence to establish a connection between program activities and life experiences.
- Being based on ownership, or having the participant help to determine what evidence to include to show that the goals are being met.
- Being multipurposed, or allowing for assessment of the effectiveness of the program while also assessing the performance of the participant.

Portfolio assessments are not as useful for the following situations:

- Evaluating programs that have very concrete, uniform purposes or goals. For instance, it would not be necessary to compile a portfolio for a programs such as immunizing children by the age of five because the immunizations are the same and the evidence is usually straightforward and clear.
- Allowing a teacher to rank participants or a program in a quantitative or standardized way, even though evaluators or staff members of the program might be able to make subjective judgments on that which is relative.
- Comparing participants or programs to standardized norms. Portfolios can and often do include some kinds of standardized test scores along with other types of evidence. However, this is not the main purpose in using portfolio assessments.

The main factors that guide the design and development of a portfolio are:

- Purpose. The primary concern is understanding the purpose that is to be served by the portfolio. This will define guidelines for collecting materials. For instance, is the goal to report progress? To identify special needs? For program accountability? For all such reasons?
- Assessment criteria. The next decision to make is about what are the criteria standards, such as what will be considered a success, and what strategies are needed to meet the goals. Items are then selected to provide evidence of meeting said criteria or making progress with respect to the goals which have been set.
- Evidence. A number of considerations in collecting data are needed. What are the sources of evidence? How often should evidence be collected? How can sense be made of the evidence?

Miscue analysis

A miscue analysis is an assessment in which a child reads a story aloud and the teacher checks for errors in the recognition and comprehension of words. Such an analysis might be performed in the following manner:

- The teacher instructs the student that they will read a passage aloud without the teacher's help.
- A videotape or audiotape should be made for analysis after the session.
- After reading the teacher marks all miscues, including insertions, mispronunciations, omissions, and corrections by the student.
- The teacher records the miscues by writing what the text said in one column and what the reader said in another.
- The miscues are analyzed using criteria, including whether the miscue went with the preceding context and whether it was corrected.
- Percentages are calculated based on the total number of miscues.

Journals

Journals let students write an ongoing record of thoughts, ideas, experiences, and reflections on a given topic. They go beyond the demands of usual written assignments as they promote integration of personal thoughts and expression with materials for a class. Journals provide a systematic means of collecting evidence and documenting learning for self-evaluation and reflections. Journals can be structured or free-form. Structured journals are when students are given specific questions, a set of guidelines, or a target on which to base their writing. Free-form lets students record thoughts and feelings with little direction. Whatever the form, journals are valuable in assessing a student's ability to observe, challenge, doubt, question, explore, and solve problems.

Validity and reliability

A test is valid when it measures what it is supposed to measure. The validity of a test depends on the purpose for which it is to be used. For instance, a thermometer might measure temperature, but it cannot measure barometric pressure. A test is reliable when it yields results that are consistent. A test may be reliable and valid, valid and unreliable, reliable and invalid, or neither valid nor reliable. A test must be reliable for it to measure validity and the validity of a test is constrained by its reliability. If a test does not consistently measure a construct or domain, then it may not be expected to have a high degree of validity.

Types of test validity include:

- Face validity. This asks the question: Does the test measure what should be measured?
- Content validity. This asks: Is the full content of the concept being defined included in the measure? It must include a broad sample of what is tested, emphasize material that is important and, require skills that are appropriate.
- Criterion validity. This asks: Is the measure consistent with what is already known and expected? There are two subcategories, which are predictive and concurrent.
- Predictive validity predicts a known association between the construct being measured and something else.
- Concurrent validity is associated with indicators that pre-exist or with something that already measures the same concept.
- Construct validity. This shows the measure that relates to a number of other measures that are specified.
- Discriminant validity. This type does not associate with unrelated constructs.

Threats to the internal validity of a test

Factors affecting how valid a test is by itself include:

- History. Outside events that happen during the course of what is being studied may influence the results. It does not make the test less accurate.
- Maturation. Change due to aging or development between or within groups may affect validity.
- Instrumentation. The reliability is questioned because of a calibration change in a measuring device or changes in human ability to measure difference, such as fatigue or experience.
- Testing. Test-taking experience affects results. This refers to either physical or mental changes, such as changes in the attitude or physiological response of a participant after repeated measures.
- Statistical regression. This is the tendency to regress towards the mean, making some scores higher or lower.

If a measure is not reliable, some variation will occur between repeated measures.

Additional threats to the internal validity of a test

A test may have the following threats to its internal validity:

- Selection. Participants in a group may be alike in certain ways, but will respond differently to the independent variable.
- Mortality. Participants drop out of a test, making the group unequal. Who drops out and why can be a factor.
- Interaction. Two or more threats can interact, such as selection-maturation when there is a difference between age groups causing groups to change at different ages.
- Contamination. This is when a comparison group in some way impacts another group, causing an increase of efforts. This is also called "compensatory rivalry."

Conventional views of test reliability

Views in recent decades on test reliability include:

- Temporal stability. This refers to implementing the same form of testing on two or more separate occasions to the same group of students. This is not practical as repeated measurements are likely to result in higher scores on later tests after students become familiar with the format.
- Form equivalence. This is relative to two different test forms based on the same content, administered once to the same group of students.
- Internal consistency. This relates to the coefficient of test scores obtained from a single test. When no pattern is found in the student responses, the test is probably too difficult and the students resorted to randomly guessing at the answers.
- Reliability is a necessary but insufficient condition for a test to be valid. The test might reflect consistent measurement but it may not be especially valid.

Conventional views of test validity

Some conventional views on test validity in recent years include:

- Face validity. This means that a test is valid at face value. As a check on face validity, psychometricians traditionally sent test items to teachers for modification. This was abandoned for a long time because of its vagueness and subjectivity. But face validity returned in the 1990s in another form, with validity defined as making common sense, being persuasive, and appearing right to the reader.
- Content validity. This draws inferences from test scores to a large domain of items that are similar to those on a test. The concern with content validity is a sample-population representation, meaning that the knowledge and skills covered by the test should be representative of the larger knowledge and skill domain.

Regression analysis with respect to test validity

Regression analysis can be used to establish validity of the criteria of a test. An independent variable may be used as a predictor of the dependent variable, which is the criterion variable. The correlation coefficient between them is known as the validity coefficient. For instance, test scores are the criterion variable. It is hypothesized that if the student passes the test, he or she would meet the criteria of knowing all the specific subject matter. Criterion validity values prediction over explanation. Prediction is concerned with mathematical or non-casual dependence, whereas explanation pertains to casual or logical dependence. For instance, one can predict the weather based on the mercury height in a thermometer. The mercury could satisfy the criterion validity as a predictor. Yet one cannot say why the weather changes because of the mercury's height.

Two sources of test invalidity

Two particular threats to test validity are known as "construct underrepresentation" and "construct-irrelevant variance." The first term indicates that the task being measured in the assessment fails to include important discussions or facets of the construct. So the test results will indicate a student's abilities within only a portion of the construct intended to be measured by the test. The second term means that a test measures too many variables. Many of these variables are irrelevant to the interpreted construct. This can take two forms. "Construct-irrelevant easiness" occurs when outside clues in format permit some individuals to respond correctly or appropriately

- 69 -

in ways which are irrelevant to the assessed construct. "Construct-irrelevant difficulty" occurs when outside aspects make it more difficult for individuals to respond correctly.

Evaluating a child for reading problems

Parents whose children are being tested for reading problems should be assured by teachers or reading specialists that the evaluation:

- Uses the native language such as Spanish or sign language unless it is clearly impossible to do so.
- Does not discriminate against the child because he or she has some type of disability or comes from a background that is racially or culturally different.
- Is administered by evaluators who know how to give the tests they decide to use.
- Will be used to determine if the child has a disability and to select the educational program that fits the child's needs. These decisions cannot be based solely on one evaluation.

Conjoint behavioral consultation

Conjoint behavioral consultation (CBC) is a partnership model of service delivery in which parents, educators, other primary caregivers, and service providers all work in collaboration to meet the developmental needs of children, address their concerns, and achieve success by promoting the competencies of all parties concerned. CBC creates an opportunity for families and schools to work together for a common interest and to build upon and promote the capabilities and strengths of the family members and school personnel. Individual needs are identified and acted upon using an organized approach that is data-based and that has mutual and collaborative interactions between parents and children, along with the guidance and assistance of consultants such as school psychologists.

Conjoint behavioral consultant partnerships (CBC) can be implemented through four stages: needs identification, needs analysis, plan development, and plan evaluation. Three of these stages use interviews to structure the decisions to be made. Overall, the goal is to effectively address needs and desires of parents and teachers for the children. Specific objectives include:

- Addressing concerns as they happen across, rather than only within, individual settings.
- Enhancing home-school partnerships to benefit student learning and performance.
- Establishing joint responsibility for solving problems.
- Improving communications between children, families, and school personnel.
- Assessing needs in a comprehensive and functional way.
- Promoting continuity and consistency among agents of change and across various settings.
- Providing opportunities for parents to become empowered using strength-based orientation.

Reading First professional development programs

Training in the five essential components of reading instruction is one of the most important elements of a quality professional development plan under the Reading First initiative. Teachers should learn effective strategies for providing explicit and systematic instruction for each component. Those components are:

- Phonemic awareness. Teachers should understand the difference between phonemic awareness and phonics. Phonemic awareness focuses on hearing sounds and learning how those sounds are put together.
- Phonics. Teachers should be trained in explicit and systematic phonics instruction based on scientifically based reading research.
- Fluency. Teachers will learn the various techniques for reading fluency, such as teacher modeling, repeating reading aloud, and choral reading.
- Reading vocabulary. Teachers can learn several effective techniques for teaching vocabulary.
- Reading comprehension. Professional development can give teachers certain comprehension strategies to help students understand what they read.

There are certain requirements for implementing federal Reading First professional development plans. They include:

- The plans must be closely aligned with the principles of scientifically-based reading research and the five essential components of reading instruction. The programs must provide instruction in scientifically-based reading instructional materials, programs, strategies, and approaches. Also, the programs must train teachers in the appropriate use of assessment tools and in the analysis and interpretation of gathered data.
- An eligible professional development provider must deliver the professional development program. To be eligible, the provider must be able to train teachers, including special education teachers, in reading instruction that is grounded in scientifically-based reading research.
- Teachers must be instructed in teaching all components of reading instruction and must understand how the components are related, the progression in which they should be taught, and the underlying structure of the English language.

Since Reading First is a federal initiative, many states may have similar state guidelines for carrying out the initiative, such as summer reading programs. Some guideline examples might include:

- The use of Reading First-approved core, supplemental, and intervention programs.
- Daily 90-minute uninterrupted reading instructional blocks. This would include systematic delivery of explicit instruction using approved core reading program material.
- Intervention services provided for students who are below the mastery of reading skills.
- Evidence of teacher's use of data to drive instruction. Reports on the program developed by the state will include information on the number of students served, the summer school teacher credentials, student achievement gain, and percentage of students meeting end of grade benchmarks at the beginning and end of the summer program.

Conveying high expectations to students

Researchers have found certain ways that a school may let students know that the school's expectations of them are high:

- Establish policies that emphasize how important it is to achieve academically. This can be done by notifying parents if students are not meeting the academic expectations or setting minimally acceptable achievement levels for students to participate in sports or extracurricular activities.
- Use slogans that communicate high expectations for the students such as "Yes we can."
- Protect instructional time and discourage tardiness, absenteeism, and interruptions.
- Provide insistent coaching to students who experience difficulty with learning tasks. Researchers say that excusing children from trying hard to succeed in academics because it is not fair or because it is hopeless to expect any more does not really help students in learning. It detracts from academic skills and can also lower motivation and self-esteem.

Problem-solving process

A problem-solving process can be used with methods to assess or measure how well the curriculum is meeting students' needs so that changes in the curriculum can be made. The process includes:

- Identify the problem to be solved. For instance, a marked underachievement in reading.
- Identify alternative solutions to the problem, such as a new reading method.
- Implement new programs and test alternative solutions. Revise unsuccessful solutions.
- Terminate the problem. This includes revising unsuccessful instructional programs. When making changes in a student's instructional program, teachers should be aware of various alterable characteristics of instruction that are under the direct control of the teacher.

Evolutionary changes and revolutionary changes

Instructional changes can be viewed as either revolutionary or evolutionary. Revolutionary changes are those with major modifications in an instructional program. Evolutionary changes are minor ones. Evolutionary changes may be made in certain parts of the instructional plan such as time, activity, materials, or motivation. A revolutionary change could include the method of instruction from a language experience approach to direct instruction. Technically sound achievement indicators for such decisions include the number of words read correctly for reading, and the number of correct letter sequences in two minutes or the number of words spelled in two minutes for spelling. For written expression, the indicators could be the number of words written, the number of correctly spelled words, or the number of correct word sequences in two minutes.

Effective curricula that are culturally responsive

- Effective curricula that are culturally responsive share certain characteristics. These include:
- The curriculum is integrated and interdisciplinary. It does not rely on one-time activities or "sprinkling" the traditional curriculum with a few minority individuals.
- It is authentic, connected to the child's real life, and child-centered. It uses materials from the child's culture and history to illustrate concepts and principles.
- It develops critical thinking skills.
- It often incorporates strategies that use cooperative learning, whole language instruction, and self-esteem building, and recognizes diverse styles of learning.

- It is supported by appropriate staff development and pre-service preparation.
- It is part of a coordinated strategy. Successful implementation requires a school climate that is receptive and the recognition that the hidden curriculum in any school can be a powerful ally or a powerful enemy.

Assessing curriculum materials for cultural relevance

A number of criteria should be evaluated when looking for curriculum materials that are culturally relevant. Teachers should look for invisibility, stereotyping, selectivity, imbalance, unreality, isolation, language bias, and fragmentation. Also to be looked for in books is the inappropriate treatment of African Americans, Native Americans, Asian Americans, and Hispanic Americans, especially when the "one size fits all view" is expressed. This is where instructional material reflects through generalization that there is a single Hispanic, African, Asian, or Native culture. The sidebar approach also should be avoided. This is where a few isolated events relevant to ethnic experiences are relegated to a box or sidebar that is set apart from the rest of the text.

Facilitator in culturally-relevant approaches to education

- A teacher can become a facilitator in transferring school knowledge to that of real life by involving a student's home culture in learning. Ways to do this include:
- Have students share artifacts from home that are reflective of their culture.
- Have students write about traditions that their families share.
- Have students research different aspects of their culture.
- Have members of the community who share a culture with your students speak to the class on various subjects.
- Involve the class in making something relevant to other cultures (such as a piñata for studying the Hispanic culture.)

Critically analyzing school wide reading programs

When critically looking at goals and needs, schools should recognize that the ultimate goal is better results. Measuring progress, being accountable for results, and making changes based on reliable data are vital aspects of school wide improvement. Many school leaders look upon this process as a work in progress. Continuous data-driven accountability involves teams of teachers and reading specialists engaging in the following activities:

- Combine information from multiple measurements on all groups of students.
- Organize data to clarify strengths and needs of the school as a whole.
- Disaggregate information on students to determine whether some subgroups are experiencing common problems.
- Keep alert to the implications of the quality of education supported by the school as a whole.

Continuous progress monitoring

Continuous monitoring that allows analysis of school wide programs such as reading gives the faculty and staff a sense of ownership by putting accountability in their hands. Few surprises exist in continuous monitoring because the school is in control of its own assessment. Teachers and school leaders score many of their own tests so they learn the results immediately. As teams of reading specialists and classroom teachers examine the data, they look for information about different aspects of the subject within the school. With data analysis, questions may be asked such as: Are there grades with an especially strong or weak showing in the subject? Are non-English or limited-English speakers improving their use of test materials?

Reading specialist

Reading specialists help staff develop knowledge of literacy theory and instructions. They are consultants and collaborating teachers for classroom teachers, aides, parents, and other teachers such as special education, speech, music, and art. Some schools have chosen to replace reading specialists with teaching assistants who lack specialized literacy training. When this happens, a grave injustice is done to students, teachers, and the literacy program. Reading specialists provide expert instruction to learners who differ in language, learning style, culture, and ability. They share effective learning strategies and practices with school staff and parents, and they serve as experts for the school and district on information about reading and literacy instruction.

Home-school connections

Schools are now opening their doors more as community resources to serve students and families. So-called "full-service" schools show that they are paying attention to the students' holistic needs as well as their academic needs. These schools offer health, counseling, social service, and other programs to support learning and growth. Some community-initiated activities are also transforming schools. These communities are taking responsibility to use information about schools to offer new ways to improve schools. They are working with schools on recurring problems. The schools are beginning to change in ways that bring more voices to the table when it comes to decision-making.

There are a number of concrete steps that community members can take to help schools improve and especially to help more children to read. Community members can:

- Become a learning partner or tutor. The citizen can tutor a child in the child's own neighborhood or in a local elementary school. Volunteers might read with or to a child for 30 minutes a week for at least eight weeks, and could also take the child to the library to get him or her a library card.
- Volunteer to serve as a community coordinator for a community reading program. A number of organizations can work to recruit tutors. This person can also work with local schools to match community members and children.
- Ask organizations to help support community reading programs. Local businesses can be encouraged to donate supplies or allow employees time off to volunteer in school.

Parental education and socioeconomic status

The exact nature of the impact parental education and social economic status has on student achievement although it does have an impact. Studies have found that parental education and family socioeconomic status alone are not necessarily predictors of how students will achieve academically. Studies have found that parental education accounts for about a quarter of the variance in student test scores while socioeconomic status accounts for slightly more than a quarter. Other research indicates that dysfunctional home environments, low expectations from parents, parenting that is ineffective, differences in language and high mobility levels may account for the low achievement levels among those students that come from lower socioeconomic levels.

Progress monitoring

Progress monitoring is a classroom-based assessment for reading instruction that evaluates how well a child is learning based upon a systematic review by teachers of children who perform academic tasks equivalent to those which are a part of the student's daily classroom instruction. Unlike a one-time test for proficiency, this type of ongoing assessment helps to determine whether students are making sufficient progress or require more help in achieving grade-level reading objectives. Progress monitoring should have certain benchmarks to ensure reliability and validity. Progress monitoring can assess the efficacy of various components of a student's instruction in reading such as in phonemic awareness, phonics, fluency, vocabulary and reading comprehension.

Socratic questioning

Socratic questioning is at the heart of critical thinking skills. It is more than just having a one-word answer or an agreement and disagreement from students. Socratic questions force students to make assumptions, sort through both relevant and irrelevant points and, additionally, explain those points. This instruction can take many different forms including:

- Raising basic issues.
- Probing beneath the surface of matters.
- Pursing areas of thought fraught with problems.
- Helping students find the structure of their own thinking.
- Helping students develop clarity, accuracy and relevance.
- Helping students make judgments by reasoning on their own.
- Helping students to think about evidence, conclusions, assumptions, implications, points of view, concepts and interpretations.

Metadiscursive

Research shows that teaching in content areas should include teaching students to be metadiscursive, meaning that they should not only be able to be part of many different discourse communities but that they should also know why and how it is that they are taking part as well as what those engagements mean for them and others in the realm of larger power relationships and social position.

This does not mean that the historical limitations in integrating content literacy should be ignored. Teaching content literacy should still focus on the knowledge and beliefs of students and teachers, which requires considering questions such as how teachers balance the notion of subject-matter literacy as a metadiscursive practice while encountering probable resistance from students who have become comfortable with the notion that content area learning is a matter of rote memory and information reproduction.

Trade books

Trade books are instructional materials written specifically for students but are not textbooks, per se. They may be used to help improve reading skills, develop knowledge of content areas and further understand the world. Trade books can be a valued complement to teaching and curriculum. They may also affect the appreciation which a student has for content-related literature. These books should not replace thorough instruction in reading skills, however. Trade books also are not an alternative to teaching concepts of content areas, but rather, these texts can help students understand concepts by putting them into an appropriate context. Teachers can use strategies such as this to help develop better reading skills and help students comprehend the text.

Dramatic activities as scaffolding for elementary and English as a second language instruction

Elementary and English as a Second Language classes can receive scaffolding for effective literacy from dramatic activities. Researchers have found that scaffolded play with students of elementary age allow them to participate in language learning in an active way. Students may also be more motivated to discuss, organize, rewrite and perform in the dramatic presentation.

Students have also become more engaged in which there were interwoven activities involving literature, drama, music and movement, even for at-risk students in grades K-3. Activities involving bilingual children in which their own cultural experiences are called upon and valued also helps motivate and support literacy and meaningful learning environments.

Learning culture

Students learning culture should be taught to react appropriately in social situations. They should be able to describe a pattern in the culture and recognize a pattern when it is illustrated. Additionally, they should be able to explain these patterns and predict how a pattern is likely to apply in a given situation. Students learning culture should describe or manifest an attitude that is important for making oneself acceptable in a foreign society. They should evaluate the form of a statement concerning a culture pattern and describe or demonstrate defensible methods of analyzing a sociocultural whole. They should identify basic human responses which signify that that which is being taught is understood.

Keeping expectations high for recent immigrant students

It is common for some teachers to become frustrated upon seeing that they are unable to reach one or more of their students. Becoming more culturally informed can help enhance the teaching repertoire. This information can also help teachers realize that these students may have trouble under the teaching of any skilled instructor. But the belief that is expressed in a student helps to create persistence and motivation on their part. Linguistic as well as academic achievements in the United States are often only realized because of the patience, tolerance and encouragement which American teachers display. Effort is promoted by teachers who are supportive and who create a valuing, welcoming and accepting educational setting.

Support services for recent immigrant students

Schools can help recent immigrants feel welcome and supported while developing positive identities that are cross-cultural. Schools have many ways to assist their students in learning the curriculum and adapting to American culture and habits. For example, a recent arrival can be partnered with another student who speaks his or her language or dialect, even if they are not necessarily of the same nationality or heritage. Cross-age tutoring is also an option that might be considered. Candidates include someone from the student's culture or region, other recent immigrants, or an accepting and helpful American youngster. Hiring paraprofessionals who speak the student's language can also be helpful.

Between-class ability approach to grouping

Between-class ability grouping is not a strategy in which all students can learn. Students at the top level seem to benefit but those in the middle and lower levels may not. It is nonetheless a popular practice in American education. The problem may lie more with the method of grouping than with the concept itself. Ability groups are mostly determined by standardized testing or basic skills tests. But students may not have uniform knowledge of, and aptitude for, the various content areas. Another problem, research demonstrates, is that teachers' expectations and the quality of instruction are often lower for lower-track groups in between-class grouping. Students may also lower their own expectations when placed in a lower-level group. This may affect self-concept in academic achievement, and thus, affect the teacher's expectations.

Combined grade classes

Combined classes are those which include more than one grade level in a classroom. These classes are sometimes referred to as split classes, blended classes or double-year classes. These classes will usually include the required curriculum for each of the two grades that are represented, yet some class activities may take place with children who are from both of the combined grades. This type of grouping takes place more frequently in smaller schools, yet on occasion in larger schools when the number of children in different age groups tends to have fluctuated. The main purpose of such classes appears to be maximizing resource use with regard to personnel and space instead of capitalizing on the diversity of ability and experience within the groups of mixed ages.

Valuing correct answers

One of the most effective points that can be made to help establish a safe learning environment for students is to emphasize that errors are friends rather than faults. Students often apologize for not knowing something. They can be reassured that no one knows everything and that everyone has something to learn. Teachers can teach them to value their correct answers rather than dwelling on the errors that they made, and point out patterns of errors as well. For example, they can be taught to count the number of questions about which they were correct, thus offering positive reinforcement. Even if a student gets one item correct and the remainder incorrect, the student can be told that they have already learned something.

Peer mediation programs

Peer mediation uses a group of student mediators who are taught a negotiation procedure that is interest-based, along with problem-solving and communicational strategies to help settle disagreements without confrontation or violent actions. Students come to mediation on a voluntary basis and are guided by the peer mediators to move from blaming one other to coming up with solutions that are acceptable to all parties. Peer mediation often is put in place as part of a broader program for conflict resolution. Peer mediation can substantially change how students approach conflicts and settle them. Students who are involved in peer mediation oftentimes express a greater desire to help friends avoid fights and solve their problems.

Alternatives to technological means and reducing student disruption

Little data exists demonstrating that punitive "zero tolerance" policies have significantly improved school safety or student behavior. Researchers have begun to discover that which is and is not efficacious in preventing school violence. The programs that seem to be most effective are proactive rather than reactive, involving families, students, teachers and communities. They include a number of components that help address the complexity of school violence and disruption. There is far more data available supporting the effectiveness of bullying prevention programs, anger management or peer mediation programs than there is to support how well violence and disruption is stemmed by technological means such as surveillance cameras or metal detectors.

Eye coordination problems

Four general types of eye coordination problems can affect a young reader -- astigmatism, eye-hand coordination, visual motor problems and other conditions, and esophoria. Children will get into postures that are distorted while trying to get one eye to function. They will often put their head down on their arms, covering an eye with their hand or rotating their head so that their nose bridge interferes with one eye's vision. Esophoria is another eye coordination problem that tends to turn eyes inward. A child will see objects smaller than they really are. The only way that a child can view the object as larger is to move it closer to him or her.

Discrepancy criteria and assumptions about unique types of poor reading

Most state and federal guidelines for identifying those with reading disabilities have as a foundation an ability-achievement discrepancy. It is usually operationalized as an IQ-achievement discrepancy. An assumption behind such guidelines has been that poor readers with discrepancies or the reading disabled, have a unique type of poor reading, different from other poor reading types. Such criteria have been attacked by reading disability researchers, who argue that there are many similarities between those who read poorly and have discrepancies and poor readers who have no discrepancies such as children whose IQs are on level with their reading ability but are not low enough for them to be termed intellectually disabled. Both groups seem to have problems with word decoding and phonological functions and little evidence is present to support the notion that poor readers with discrepancies can eventually perform better than those with none.

Assumptions of intrinsic processing disorder and processing tests

An educational diagnosis of reading disorders normally employs processing tests, which test memory, language ability, and visual and auditory processing. Poor readers do have certain difficulties in certain processing measures such as decoding words and phonological processing. These tests can provide early identification of reading problems and also help plan an educational program for the student. The problem is that word decoding and phonological processing measures are not always emphasized in identification of reading disabilities in schools. Many such measures lack validity and reliability and interpretations of these tests also present problems. A poor performance on these tests is most often interpreted as evidence of a processing disorder intrinsic to the reader, but researchers emphasize that processing is shaped not only by innate characteristics such as genetics but also experiences such as reading in class.

Scoring an informal reading inventory

Once written comprehension questions are chosen, a teacher will want to determine the number of errors that are permissible for the students. Students are often graded and grouped into three categories: independent (the student can read on their own), instructional (the student could read if classroom help is available) and frustration (the student will most likely find this piece too difficult even in a classroom setting). Where the child falls on that scale depends upon the amount of errors per 100 words that the student commits. For example, an "independent" reader might commit one or two errors per 100 words and score 90 percent or higher on comprehension questions.

Running records

Running records give teachers an important tool for making decisions on appropriate grouping, materials and support when taken over time in early literacy training. They are based on structured observations of children's reading and writing behaviors and exemplify authentic assessment which is critical with emergent readers as they come across new reading material.

The student reads from a text and the teacher watches closely, coding behaviors on a sheet of paper. Words that are accurately read are given a check. Errors receive a line with reader behaviors recorded above the line and teacher actions recorded below. A goal of the running records for this level would be to help students develop a "self-extending" system, which indicates that children learn to apply strategies of self-monitoring and self-correction on more difficult texts for extended amounts of text.

Certain points should be remembered when taking and scoring running records. These include:

- Running records must be analyzed to offer data for instructional use in addition to being scored.
- Consider what text the student read, up to and including the error when analyzing a substitution.
- Do not make professional judgments base on the results of one running record. Reviewing the analysis and accuracy of scores of a number of running records is the only way to understand a student's reading process.
- Individual errors are studied for gaining insight into the reader's process.
- When analyzing a record, circle the cues that the reader used and not the ones that were neglected.

Observation

Observation is one of the most powerful techniques that a teacher has. The purpose is to build a picture of a student's personal, social and cognitive development and how they are making progress in their learning. Only when a number of cameos, vignettes, snapshots, notes or indicators exist can teachers start looking for patterns in student behavior and make judgments about their performance. Dating such records will help record the contexts along with observed achievement characteristics in order to build a historical profile that is useful. Supporting and acknowledging students working at different levels requires flexibility and tailoring to the individual student. The formats should suit the particular activities, reflect the activities' goals and support the recording of different levels and rates of students' work.

Reliability of performance, portfolio, and responsive evaluations

Some scholars and testing experts argue that performance, portfolio and responsive evaluations -- where tasks vary greatly from student to student and where multiple tasks may be simultaneously evaluated -- are not reliable. A difficulty cited is that there are more than one source of errors in measuring performance assessment. For instance, a writing skill test score might have its reliability affected by graders, or other such factors. There may also be confusion about diversity of reliability indices. Nonetheless, different reliability measures share a common thread. One such commonality is constituted in measurement procedures in situations such as internal consistency. Oftentimes for convenience in computing, the reliability index is based upon a single data collection. The ultimate reference, however, should go beyond just one testing occasion to other such occasions.

Performance factors that reading specialists might look at in consultation with teachers

Teachers may look for specific performance factors that can be passed along to the reading specialist or others for assessment in order to decide if a child needs modified reading instruction. These factors are:

- Continuous improvement. Are the student's grades improving, stagnating or declining?
- Comparative performance. Do the results show that the student is doing well in comparison to other children in comparable settings?
- Absolute performance. Do the results show the student is reaching the school's desired level of performance?
- Small-group performance. Do the results show that children of a similar group as the student (limited English, Title I students) are making better progress that that of the student in question?

Student peer training

Students have long had informal, untrained peer helping networks. Students share their concerns with each other naturally while at lunch, after school and while talking on the phone at home. The seriousness of the problems discussed have changed somewhat in today's world. Students may likely know someone who was pregnant or suicidal, who had a drug problem, was being abused or who had an eating disorder but many of these students with such problems do not seek adult help, resulting in a crisis in which a student's coping mechanisms are not effective and thus many students in the end obtain little or no help from professionals. Peer programs offer the ability to increase the student's skill in responding and helping friends, and train students to know when there is a crisis and to whom the peer may be referred.

Curriculum-based assessment

Instructional strategies are not fail-proof with regard to teaching students new skills. There are, however, a number of data-based strategies that have been identified that when used with an objective and systematic assessment can lead to a curriculum that will help improve student performance. Such an assessment is termed a curriculum-based assessment. These are models of assessment that emphasize a direct relationship to the student's curriculum. These assessments use measures from the curriculum to evaluate the effectiveness of instruction and what changes to the instruction can lead to more effective teaching methods and improved student achievement. The assessment provides information on how the student's behavior changes on a generic task of constant difficulty. Increases in the behavior being measured on equivalent forms of the task would represent growth academically.

Data sources to critically analyze school wide programs

Data sources such as aligned instructional benchmarks and assessments can be used to critically analyze school wide programs such as reading so that appropriate changes can be made to meet students' goals and needs. Many schools have linked aligned instructional benchmarks to broader objectives that are periodically measured by their state's assessment programs. Schools, through aligned assessments, can examine results for several purposes to track absolute progress, compare against benchmark goals and to find patters that reveal progress or weaknesses over time. An ongoing analysis of data can determine adjustments that are timely. Aligned information can let educators examine instructional variations that might make a difference in academic achievements.

This allows educators to ask what should be done at various levels within the classroom or school to prevent problems identified by the data.

Promoting collaboration among colleagues

The reading specialist in a school setting provides a wide variety of services, many of which are in a collaborative effort with colleagues. The specialist works with teachers to promote and develop the literacy program as well as developing thinking strategies in the classroom. As a diagnostician, the specialist administers both group and individual evaluations of reading achievement and recommends activities to build comprehension. For intervention, the specialist works with teachers as well as students and small groups for providing instruction and for building competencies in literacy. In addition, the reading specialist works with the staff and parents in order to promote various events in order to gather support for the literacy program and which support literacy as a whole.

Parental expectations and children's classroom outcomes

Various research has found that parental expectations have a significant impact upon school performance as well as being critical to achievement in academics. High expectations from parents are usually found in association with higher levels of educational attainment. Parenting practices that are effective and associated with high levels of academic achievement include expectations that children receive high numerical grades of their schoolwork. Additionally, research indicates that child rearing beliefs, ways to academically enrich home environments and standards of behavior that are acceptable both in and out of school are likewise important to achieving academically. Insofar as behavior is concerned, the children who succeed have greater adaptability to conforming with behavioral standards at school; something many have already learned through parental expectations.

Reading poetry

Some general guidelines for reading poetry may be summarized as follows:

- Understand the relationship of the title to the work. Does the title suggest anything about the subject?
- Ascertain who the "speaker" of the poem is. Determine what type of narrative is employed.
- Know the major theme or argument which dominates the work.
- Poems deal with private or individual matters or subjects in the public spectrum. Determine which the poem is addressing.
- What type of meter is used in the poem? Is rhyme employed as a device?
- Carefully examine the poem for figurative language and note how it is used.
- Be aware of the poems historical and cultural setting in order to place the meaning in context.
- Notice whether the poem fits a formally defined genre within poetry.

Oral questioning

One easy way for teachers to conduct a formative assessment in class is to briefly quiz students on the material covered. Indeed, whether it is to be done for a grade or not, it is generally useful to recapitulate the previous day's lesson at the beginning of class. Oftentimes, this can be best accomplished by allowing students to articulate the material, and to critique one another's understanding. Some probing questions from the teacher can ensure that the recent material is understood in the context of the material that has already been learned. It is not always necessary to formally grade students on their participation or performance in an informal question-and-answer session; the main thing is to develop an idea of the students' progress.

GACE Practice Test

Questions 1-10 pertain to the following passage:

The benefits of progressive education cannot be ignored in view of the problems caused by the standards-based education system. The possible advantages of the No Child Left Behind reform do little to justify the system that supports it. The progressive education that functioned in the United States through much of the late 19th and 20th centuries provided students with a sound learning foundation. Today, schools that embrace progressive techniques indicate long-term success for students. Progressive schools allow for students to learn based on their own strengths, building on knowledge over time. What is more, teachers are encouraged to utilize a variety of procedures and materials to engage students in the learning process. Standards-based education, on the other hand, focuses solely on successful testing and does not provide the effective acquisition of real knowledge.

1. Identify the main idea of the passage.
    a. Standards-based education has no value
    b. Progressive education is of more value than standards-based education
    c. The historical tradition of progressive education makes it more valid
    d. Testing has no value in education

2. Identify the author's purpose in the passage.
    a. To teach
    b. To contemplate
    c. To report
    d. To persuade

3. How does the author indicate the value of progressive education?
    a. By chronology
    b. By suggestion
    c. By example
    d. By definition

4. Identify the type of organization that the author uses in the passage?
    a. Cause and effect
    b. Clarification
    c. Spatial
    d. Comparison and contrast

5. What method of organization is used in the sentence: "Today, schools that embrace progressive techniques indicate long-term success for students"?
    a. Chronology
    b. Description
    c. Justification
    d. Simplification

- 83 -

6. The author mentions the No Child Left Behind reform as connected to which of the following types of education?

    a. Progressive education

    b. Traditional education

    c. Modern education

    d. Standards-based education

7. Identify the meaning of the expression "real knowledge" within the context of the passage.

    a. Valuable Learning

    b. Traditional Schooling

    c. Impactful Education

    d. True Illumination

8. Which of the following best describes the author's tone?

    a. Scholarly and informative

    b. Persistent and compassionate

    c. Excited and optimistic

    d. Resigned and antagonistic

9. How does the author indicate the negative qualities of standards-based education?

    a. Lack of useful testing and need for organization

    b. Focus on testing and lack of variety

    c. Importance of student direction in presenting information

    d. Lack of time-honored techniques to prove effectiveness

10. Does the passage indicate an evidence of preference on the author's part?

    a. Yes

    b. No

Questions 11-18 pertain to the following passage:

> With the rise of bilingual education initiatives throughout the United States, the English-only movement has once again become a subject of public debate. This is not the first occasion the English-only movement has made an appearance in the United States and probably will not be the last. In fact, English-only considerations seem to grow in public preferences whenever mainstream English-speaking Americans encounter a non-English-speaking culture in large numbers: with French speakers after the Louisiana Purchase, with Spanish speakers after the Mexican-American War, with Hawaiians after the acquisition of the Kingdom of Hawaii. Even German speakers were ostracized in the United States during World War I.
>
> Despite the English-only push from certain quarters, teachers and language professionals caution that it will cause more harm than good. Educators warn that English will always be the primary language of the United States, so making it a legal requirement simply alienates other cultures unnecessarily. The Linguistic Society of America argues that insisting on English as the only accepted language also fails to acknowledge the way that the English language has developed – by adopting words from a variety of other languages. Additionally, some fear that the laws requiring English as the primary language will be poorly and far too rigidly interpreted. Examples of students penalized for speaking other languages on school buses or

with friends in school hallways between classes give reason to worry about the feasibility of any English-only legislation.

11. According to the author, when do English-only movements arise?

a. When people begin to fear the influences of other cultures in the United States
b. During wartime, when the United States is involved in a conflict with a non-English-speaking nation
c. When the United States acquires a territory that includes large numbers of non-English speaking people living within it
d. Whenever there is a cultural conflict with a large group of non-English-speaking peoples in the United States

12. The passage is primarily concerned with doing which of the following?

a. Explaining the problems of the English-only movement
b. Considering the motivation behind the English-only movement, as well as the arguments against it
c. Examining the evidence on both sides of the English-only movement and arriving at a conclusion
d. Considering the modern English-only movement with past movements and predicting future English-only movements

13. Which of the following best describes the organization of the first paragraph of the passage?

a. Chronology
b. Comparison and contrast
c. Explanation
d. Clarification

14. Which of the following best describes the organization of the passage as a whole?

a. Spatial
b. Definition
c. Cause and effect
d. Chronology

15. Who does the author describe as initiating current English-only legislation?

a. Mainstream speakers of English in the United States
b. State legislations in areas where there are large numbers of speakers of other languages than English
c. Educators who support the idea that children learn best without outside linguistic influences
d. The author does not say

16. Which of the following best describes the author's tone toward the English-only movement?

a. Pessimistic
b. Enthusiastic
c. Cautious
d. Angry

17. The author indicates that the attitude of teachers and linguists toward English-only legislation is one of:

    a. General concern
    b. Outright rejection
    c. Angry disbelief
    d. Potential acceptance

18. Which of the following best describes the author's overall conclusion about the English-only movement in the United States?

    a. The English-only movement has caused a considerable amount of harm for certain groups in the United States and cannot be embraced without causing further problems
    b. Despite naysayers, the English-only movement provides an important glimpse into American culture and cannot be ignored as a force in legislation
    c. The English-only movement is popular largely among fringe groups and has real little real application within American life
    d. The English-only movement arises during specific times in American history but seems to lend itself to professional concerns and impractical legislation

Questions 19-20 pertains to the following passage:

Educators began applying behavioral techniques to education as early as the nineteenth century. It was the theories of B.F. Skinner in the mid-twentieth century, though, that sealed the influence of behaviorism in the American education system. Skinner argued against moral training and instead claimed that human behavior is simply a function of reinforcement. He also suggested that instruction is most effective when students do not fear failure and resulting punishment. Skinner recommended the use of positive reinforcement, with information provided in small but useful steps, as well as frequent praise to remove fear from students and provide as welcoming a learning environment as possible. However interesting Skinner's theories were, his claims about human behavior seem to make human beings a little less human.

19. According to the author, what did Skinner see as a major hindrance to effective learning in students?

    a. Need for useful behavioral training
    b. Anxiety about the penalties for being wrong
    c. Lack of constant praise during the learning process
    d. A welcoming learning environment for all students

20. Which sentence in the passage indicates a suggestion of bias on the author's part?

    a. "Educators began...nineteenth century"
    b. "It was...education system"
    c. "Skinner recommended...as possible"
    d. "However interesting...less human"

Questions 21-22 pertains to the following passage:

The earliest form of the alphabet that we use today is usually attributed to the Phoenician people. The Phoenicians were ancient traders who lived and worked along the Mediterranean Sea. Their extensive connections with people outside

Phoenicia, and particularly in Greece, led them to standardize their writing with an alphabet.

Many historians know, however, that the Phoenicians were not necessarily the first to develop the idea of an alphabet. The people of ancient Egypt created hieroglyphics, or pictures that represented different letters in their language. Additionally, writing has been found in the areas of Palestine and Sinai, and it indicates another early script that pre-dates the Phoenicians that might have influenced their alphabet.

21. The teacher asks the students to describe the main point of the passage they have just read. Assuming the following answer choices come from the students, which is most correct?

    a. To explain that people before the Phoenicians had been using alphabets
    b. To show that the Phoenicians stole their alphabet from earlier people
    c. To describe the way that the alphabet has developed over the years
    d. To explain that the trading the Phoenicians did affected their need for an alphabet

22. The teacher wants students to be able to understand the meaning of words based on the context of the passage. How might the teacher ask for students to deduce the meaning of the word "script"?

    a. Ask students to consider words that have a similar structure
    b. Ask students to think about the main topic of the passage and how this word might relate to it
    c. Ask students to focus on the shift in thought that occurs between the first paragraph and the second
    d. Ask students to split the word into individual sounds and deduce its meaning phonetically

Questions 23-25 pertain to the following passage:

Photosynthesis is the process that occurs when plants use sunlight to convert carbon dioxide into energy. When humans exhale, they release carbon dioxide into the atmosphere, and the plants then take this in and use it for food. Photosynthesis allows plants to use what is in the air to make their own food for survival. As plants begin to create energy from the carbon dioxide, they release oxygen back into the atmosphere. Humans then use this oxygen when they inhale. As a result, photosynthesis is a vital process that keeps the delicate balance between carbon dioxide and oxygen and allows both plants and animals to survive.

23. The teacher asks students to discuss this passage in groups. The groups are to consider the main point of the passage. Which of the following answers is most correct?

    a. Photosynthesis is the process that plants use to turn carbon dioxide into food, with the help of sunlight
    b. Without photosynthesis, humans could not survive on the earth, because photosynthesis creates oxygen
    c. Photosynthesis allows plants to make their own food and keeps them alive without the help of humans
    d. Photosynthesis is an important process that provides plants with food and helps keep a balance in the atmosphere

- 87 -

24. The teacher wants to make sure that students understand the importance of the balance of carbon dioxide and oxygen that occurs with photosynthesis. What question might the teacher ask about the passage to ensure that students appreciate this point?

    a. How can we define photosynthesis, based on the passage that I have just read?
    b. In addition to sunlight, what else do plants use to make their own food?
    c. How do humans and plants work together to ensure a healthy atmosphere?
    d. Why do plants need carbon dioxide from humans in order to survive?

25. The teacher wants to encourage students to think beyond the passage and consider how essential photosynthesis is for the survival of all life forms on earth. How might the teacher prompt students to get them to use the information from the passage and analyze beyond it?

    a. Ask students what might happen if there were not enough plants to release oxygen
    b. Develop a tree-planting project and encourage each student to plant a tree to improve the environment
    c. Have students draw a picture showing how photosynthesis works
    d. Tell students a story that shows how photosynthesis improves the life of both plants and humans

Questions 26-28 pertain to the following passage/story:

> Akhenaten was a powerful pharaoh, or king, of Egypt. He was born with the name Amenhotep, but he changed his name to Akhenaten to reflect his favorite god Aten, who was connected to the worship of the sun. Akhenaten was so devoted to Aten that he decided to change the religious system within Egypt, and during his reign Egypt became a monotheistic society; in other words, Egyptians began to worship the one god Aten. Akhenaten's queen was the beautiful Nefertiti, and he thought so highly of her that he built monuments showing her alongside him in power. At a time when pharaohs were revered as gods in their own right, this was unusual. Akhenaten is the only pharaoh known to have placed his queen beside him as an equal. As a result of his choices and the changes that he made, Akhenaten remains one of Egypt's most unique and memorable pharaohs.

26. The teacher wants the students to be able to apply basic reading skills to the passage they are studying, so the teacher quizzes the students on the word "monotheistic". Breaking this word down, the teacher asks students to identify how "mono" functions in this word:

    a. Root word
    b. Prefix
    c. Suffix
    d. Syllable

27. The teacher also wants the students to be able to make accurate inferences based on information they are studying. Considering this passage carefully, which of the following inferences can students make regarding the monotheism that Akhenaten brought to Egypt during his reign?

    a. Egypt was the only monotheistic society in the world
    b. Before Akhenaten, monotheism did not exist among ancient societies
    c. The monotheism that Akhenaten introduced was popular among the Egyptian people
    d. Before Akhenaten, the Egyptians had worshipped many gods

- 88 -

28. To explain the distinction between the monotheistic system that Akhenaten introduced and the previous religious system in Egypt, the teacher explains to students that Egypt had been polytheistic, or had worshipped many gods. The teacher then explains that these words are opposites. Which concept is the teacher describing to students?

    a. Synonyms
    b. Homonyms
    c. Antonyms
    d. Consonants

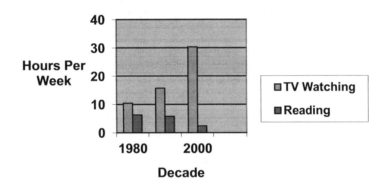

29. Which of the following best explains the information presented in the chart above?

    a. The variety of educational material on video has contributed to increased TV viewing among elementary children
    b. Reading has decreased dramatically over the course of three decades
    c. While reading has decreased over the last two decades, TV watching among elementary children has more than doubled
    d. Publishers of children's books have failed to provide reading material that captures the interest of children like TV programs do

30. The teacher provides students with a more advanced passage of reading, in which there are a variety of new words that many of the students do not know how to pronounce. How might the teacher go about helping the students in pronouncing the new words?

    a. Hint at the correct pronunciation with a variety of different rhyming words
    b. Assist the students in sounding out the words phonetically, by recognizing rules for vowels and consonants
    c. Have the students look up the words in a dictionary to review the pronunciation information that is provided there
    d. Ask students who are already familiar with the words to a help their classmates in pronouncing the new words

31. In a graduating high school class of 532, 15% of the students will receive As and 55% of the students will receive Bs. If 53 students receive Ds and no one failed, what approximate percentage of the students received Cs?

    a. 10%
    b. 20%
    c. 30%
    d. 40%

32. 37% of 461 can be rounded to which of the following?

    a. 168
    b. 169
    c. 171
    d. 172

33. 3-2/3 ÷ 5-1/3 =

    a. 3/11
    b. 7/11
    c. 11/16
    d. 15/16

34. 5/6 ÷ 3/7 x 5/9 =

    a. 6/5
    b. 1-1/6
    c. 135/129
    d. 175/162

35. Don is planning to buy a new computer that costs $700. A local store has marked the computer he would like to buy down by 15%. Additionally, Don has a coupon for a further 10% off. How much will Don save off the original list price?

    a. $140.75
    b. $157.00
    c. $164.50
    d. $175.00

36. 19% =

    a. 0.19
    b. 1.9
    c. 0.019
    d. 1.09

37. Anne is two inches taller than Morris, who is 1 inch shorter than Aiden. If Anne = x, Morris = y, and Aiden = z, which inequality best describes their heights?

    a. y > x > z
    b. z > y > x
    c. x > y > z
    d. x > z > y

38. $f(x) = x^4 + 2x^3 + 4x - 1$, when $x = -3$
   a. 12
   b. 14
   c. 23
   d. 26

39. In the number 1492.738, what is the place value of the number 3?
   a. Tenths
   b. Hundredths
   c. Thousandths
   d. Ten-thousandths

40. Due to the outbreak of illness, only 75% of the students were in class at Monroe Middle School on Thursday. If there were 834 students who attended class on Thursday, how many students total are there in the school?
   a. 1004
   b. 1008
   c. 1110
   d. 1112

41. $(4 + 6)3 =$
   a. 10
   b. 100
   c. 1000
   d. 10000

42. Identify the missing term from the following series: 1/6, 1/12, 1/18, 1/24, ____, 1/36
   a. 1/27
   b. 1/30
   c. 1/33
   d./ 1/42

43. $(-0.19) \times (0.23) =$
   a. -0.0437
   b. -0.0439
   c. -0.0521
   d. -0.0547

44. 2/3 ___ 5/6
   a. >
   b. =
   c. <
   d. Impossible to determine

45. $(4x + 3)(4x - 3) =$
   a. $16x^2 - 9$
   b. $16x^2 + 9$
   c. $16x^2 + 12x - 9$
   d. $16x^2 - 12x + 9$

46. It usually takes 7 workers a total of 10 hours to clean the stately home Duncombe Park in North Yorkshire. Illness has caused several of the workers to be unavailable, so now the cleaning of Duncombe Park takes 14 hours. How many people are now available to clean the house?

a. 3
b. 4
c. 5
d. 6

47. Ariadne drives 456 miles in 9 hours. Using the formula d = rt, which of the following best represents her approximate speed as she drives?

a. 45 mi/hr
b. 50 mi/hr
c. 55 mi/hr
d. 60 mi/hr

48. If the area of a right triangle is 20 ft2, which of the following represent the possible measurements for the base and height of the triangle?

a. B = 4 ft; H = 5 ft
b. B = 10 ft; H = 2 ft
c. B = 8 ft; H = 5 ft
d. B = 15 ft; H = 3 ft

49. A yoga facility has four studios, labeled A, B, C, and D, where the studio can hold classes concurrently. At 5 PM, the facility has four classes, with the following number of students in each class: Studio A,15 students; Studio B, 23 students; Studio C, 8 students; and Studio D, 14 students. What is the mean class size for students attending yoga classes at 5 PM?

a. 18
b. 21
c. 10
d. 15

50. Perdita is planning to prepare a recipe for a traditional English trifle. While reviewing the recipe, she notices that it calls for 350 grams of fruit. If one ounce is equal to about 28 grams, which of the following is the approximate amount of fruit in ounces that Perdita will need?

a. 9 ounces
b. 11 ounces
c. 12 ounces
d. 15 ounces

Questions 51-52 are based on the following classroom scenario:

> The instructor is helping students find the perimeter of a rectangle, where the width is 10 feet and the height is 15 feet.

51. Which of the following equations is correct for finding the perimeter of the rectangle?

a. 10 x 15
b. 10 x 10 x 15 x 15
c. (10 + 10)(15 + 15)
d. 2(10) + 2(15)

52. The students arrive at a variety of answers for the perimeter of the rectangle. Which of the following is correct?

    a. 40

    b. 50

    c. 60

    d. 65

53. Which of the following is true if $x = -\frac{2}{3}$?

I. $-3x > -2 + \frac{5}{6x}$

II. $3x^2 - 3 \le 12x + 4$

III. $|x| > 1$

    a. I only

    b. I and III

    c. II and III

    d. I, II, and III

54. For two points $(4, 2)$ and $(3, 5)$, what is the slope of a line going through both?

    a. -1

    b. 4

    c. -3

    d. 5

55. The instructor asks the students to solve the following volume equation. For a right cylinder with a diameter of 6 and a height of 12, what is the volume that it can hold?

    a. 84π

    b. 96π

    c. 100π

    d. 108π

Questions 56-57 pertains to the following chart:

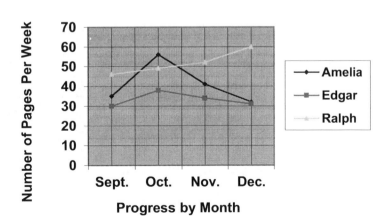

56. Due to concerns about the reading progress among several students, the instructor began charting the average number of pages that the students were reading on a weekly basis. The chart above shows the results over a four-month period, from September through December. Which of the following can be deduced from the information provided in the chart?

    a. Amelia gradually improved in her reading progress from September through December
    b. The improvement in Edgar's reading was clearly halted by a personal situation in November
    c. Ralph is the only student that consistently increased his reading from September through December
    d. This chart does not provide enough detail to show the reading progress of all three students from September through December

57. According to the chart, approximately how many pages per week did Amelia read during the month of December?

    a. 25
    b. 30
    c. 40
    d. 45

58. Students are given the following word problem and are asked to convert it to numbers and symbols: divide the product of seven and six by the sum of three and four. What is the correct way to write this with numbers and symbols?

    a. (7 x 6)/(3 + 4)
    b. (3 + 4)/(7 + 6)
    c. (7 + 6)/(3 + 4)
    d. (7 x 6)/(3 x 4)

59. Which formula shown below is the correct formula for finding the area of the following polygon?

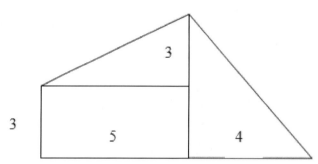

    a. (3 x 5)/2 + (3 x 5) + (4 x 6)/2
    b. 2(3 x 5) + (4 x 6)/2
    c. (3 x 5) + (3 x 6)/x + (4 x 6)
    d. (5 x 6) + (4 x 6)/2

60. The instructor gives students the following word problem:

    According to legend, when Queen Dido first arrived in the place that would become the city of Carthage, she requested the land to build the city. She was told that she could have as much land as could fit within the area of a small piece of animal skin. Not to be outdone, Dido then proceeded to cut the piece of animal skin into tiny pieces and outline the perimeter of the city that she would build – thus making the city considerably larger than the area of animal skin that she was given! If the animal skin was in the shape of a rectangle and measured 3 feet by 4 feet, and if Dido cut the tiny pieces into equal strips of 1 inch along the shorter side by two inches along the longer side, how many would she have for the perimeter of the city that she built?

a. 120
b. 365
c. 578
d. 864

This passage contains a variety of errors. Read carefully, and then review the questions that follow. Each of the questions reproduces a sentence or sentences from the passage with a selection of underlined words. Identify the <u>error</u> that is underlined, or select the answer choice for "The sentence is correct." Questions 61-65 pertain to the following passage:

Although the story of Robin Hood is often considered to be legend, many scholars argue that the legend has some fact to it. Thirteenth-century legal documents refers to a "Robinhood" who is described as something of a common, and very successful, thief. After this, the ballads of the thirteenth and fourteenth centuries provide something of a legendery story for him. It is in these ballads that Robin Hood and his Merry Men of Sherwood Forest begin to make an appearance. Over time, the story came to take on other characters as well. Maid Marian and Friar Tuck would became part of the story in the fifteenth century and beyond.

Despite the historical confidence from some scholars, others disagree about the validity of the story. Those who study mythology tend to argue that the story, itself is just a part of myth and cannot be assumed to be anything but pure fantasy. Some concede that the legend might have the more vague of historical origins, but those who oppose a root in reality tend to believe that the story is purely mythology and should be enjoyed as such.

61. Thirteenth-century legal documents <u>refers</u> to a "Robinhood" <u>who</u> is described as <u>something</u> of a common, and very successful, thief.

   a. refer
   b. whom
   c. somewhat
   d. The sentence is correct

62. After this, the ballads of the thirteenth and fourteenth centuries <u>provide</u> something of a <u>legendery</u> story for <u>him</u>.

   a. provides
   b. legendary
   c. he
   d. The sentence is correct

63. Over time, the story came <u>to take on</u> other characters as well. Maid Marian and Friar Tuck <u>would became</u> part of the story in the <u>fifteenth century</u> and beyond.

  a. took on
  b. would become
  c. fifteenth-century
  d. The sentence is correct

64. Those who study mythology <u>tend to argue</u> that the <u>story, itself</u> is just a part of <u>myth and</u> cannot be assumed to be anything but pure fantasy.

  a. tends to argue
  b. story itself
  c. myth, and
  d. The sentence is correct

65. <u>Some concede</u> that the legend might have the <u>most vague</u> of historical origins, but those <u>who</u> oppose a root in reality tend to believe that the story is purely mythology and should be enjoyed as such.

  a. Some conceded
  b. more vague
  c. whom
  d. The sentence is correct

Question 66 pertain to the following:

> Many of the Arthurian legends are believed to have come from the writings of twelfth-century *trouvère* Chretien de Troyes.

66. A word's part of speech can be recognizable, even if it's meaning is unknown. In the sentence above, what is the part of speech of the word *trouvère,* based on its context in the sentence?

  a. noun
  b. verb
  c. adjective
  d. adverb

Question 67 pertains to the following:

> Many literary scholars also point to the traditions of the Welsh story collection known as the *Mabinogion* for the origins. And even the name of the legendary King Arthur.

67. The statements above exhibit which of the following grammatical errors?

  a. Incorrectly placed comma
  b. Incorrect use of capitalization
  c. Incomplete sentence
  d. There is no error

Question 68 pertains to the following:

> For modern readers, the stories contained within the Arthurian legends are often most familiar because of English poet Alfred, Lord Tennyson, his *Idylls of the King* focuses largely on the romantic triangle of Arthur, Guinevere, and Lancelot.

68. The sentence above exhibits which of the following grammatical errors?

    a. Comma splice

    b. Incorrect verb tense

    c. Incorrect use of parallelism

    d. There is no error

Question 69 pertains to the following:

> While set in the ancient and mythical world of Camelot, Tennyson's *Idylls of the King* often do more to reflect the Victorian issues of his day than to enlighten the reader about the world of King Arthur.

69. In the sentence above, the expressions "to reflect" and "to enlighten" are examples of which of the following types of verbals?

    a. adverb

    b. gerund

    c. participle

    d. infinitive

70. Which of the following words is <u>not</u> spelled correctly?

    a. liaison

    b. definitely

    c. relevant

    d. accomodate

This passage contains a variety of errors. Read carefully, and then review the questions that follow. Each of the questions reproduces a sentence or sentences from the passage with a selection of underlined words. Identify the error that is underlined, or select the answer choice for "The sentence is correct."

Questions 71-78 pertain to the following passage:

> Today, history remembers Tsar Ivan IV of Russia as "Ivan Grozny," or "Ivan the Terrible." Scholars are in disagreement about just *how* terrible Ivan was but they do agree that his reign is one of the most significant in Russian history. Ivan was born into a tumultuous period. On the night of his birth, soothsayers prophesy that his life and reign will bring darkness upon Russia. When Ivan was only three years old, his father Grand Prince Vasili III died, leaving the Russian nobles to vie for power in the Russian court. Ivan's mother Yelena was poisoned when he was only eight years old, and when Ivan was fourteen he finally through off the authority of the nobles, called *boyars*, and took power for himself.a
>
> Many of Ivan the Terribles reforms brought positive change to Russia. Ivan attempted to modernize sixteenth-century Russia and improve its legal code, as well as increase building projects that would place Russia firm in the position of a world power. With the greater power for Russia, though, also came greater power for the ruler, Ivan was the first to take the official and permanent title of "tsar." (Which his grandfather Ivan III had first used intermittently.) Historian argue that over time the increased power began to influence Ivan's behavior to the point that he became paranoid, and unstable. One night, he attacked his pregnant daughter in law, causing her to lose her child, and when his son confronted him, Ivan attacked and killed his

son. After Ivan's death in 1584, the Russian throne would pass to at least seven different rulers in less than fifteen years, and it would not be until the accession of Mikhail Romanov in 1596, that Russia would regain stability.

71. Scholars <u>are in disagreement</u> about just how terrible Ivan <u>was but</u> they do agree that his reign is one of the most significant in <u>Russian history</u>.

    a. is in disagreement
    b. was, but
    c. Russian History
    d. There is no error

72. On the night of his <u>birth</u>, soothsayers <u>prophesy</u> that his life and reign <u>would bring</u> darkness upon Russia.

    a. birth
    b. prophesied
    c. will bring
    d. There is no error.

73. Ivan's mother Yelena was poisoned when <u>he was</u> only eight years old, and when Ivan was fourteen he finally <u>through off</u> the authority of the nobles, called *boyars*, and took power for <u>himself</u>.

    a. he is
    b. threw off
    c. him
    d. There is no error

74. Many of Ivan the <u>Terribles</u> <u>reforms</u> brought positive <u>change</u> to Russia.

    a. Terrible's
    b. reform
    c. changes
    d. There is no error

75. Ivan attempted to modernize <u>sixteenth-century Russia</u> and improve its legal <u>code, as well</u> as increase building projects that would <u>place Russia firm</u> in the position of a world power.

    a. sixteenth century Russia
    b. code as well as
    c. place Russia firmly
    d. There is no error

76. (Which his grandfather Ivan III had first used intermittently.)

The sentence above exhibits which of the following grammatical errors?

    a. Incorrectly used adverb
    b. Incomplete sentence
    c. Incorrect capitalization
    d. There is no error

77. <u>Historians</u> argue <u>that over time</u> the increased power began to influence Ivan's behavior to the point that he became <u>paranoid, and</u> unstable.

    a. Historian
    b. that, over time,
    c. paranoid and
    d. There is no error

78. <u>One night,</u> he attacked his pregnant <u>daughter in law,</u> causing her to lose her child, and when his son confronted him, Ivan <u>attacked and</u> killed his son.

    a. One night
    b. daughter-in-law
    c. attacked, and
    d. There is no error

79. One of Mikhail Romanov's most famous heirs is Peter the Great. Who is renowned for the enormous modernization that he brought to Russia and for the construction of the city of Saint Petersburg.

Which of the following changes will best correct the grammatical error in the sentence above?

    a. ...Peter the Great who is renowned...
    b. ...to Russia, and for the construction...
    c. ...the city of St. Petersburg
    d. The sentence needs no correction

80. The Romanov dynasty ended in 1917 when the last tsar, Nicholas II, was forced to abdicate. Nicholas, his wife Alexandra, and their five children were then placed in captivity, and in 1918, they were brutally murdered by Bolshevik revolutionaries.

Which of the following changes will best correct the grammatical error in the sentences above?

    a. ...ended in 1917, when the last tsar...
    b. ...his wife Alexandra and their five children...
    c. ...murdered by bolshevik revolutionaries
    d. The sentences need no correction

Directions for Questions 81-85: In each of the questions below, there are four underlined selections. Next to each underlined portion is a letter that corresponds to an answer choice on the answer sheet, (A), (B), (C), or (D). Select the letter that is next to the error. This may be an error in spelling, punctuation, word choice, and grammatical construction. Note that each sentence contains only one error.

81. Although William Wordsworth is usually remember [A] as the first major Romantic poet, some scholars [B] look to William Blake as one of the most [C] important early figures in Romanticism [D].

82. William Blake was [A] certainly unique for his time; an engraver by trade, Blake is [B] known for having illustrated [C] a number of different copies for much [D] of his poems.

83. One [A] of Blake's most creative works is the collection [B] of poetry known as *Visions of the Daughters of Albion*, which still mystify [C] literary scholars [D] to this day.

84. More [A] famous, perhaps, is Blake's popular poem "*The Tiger.*" While often anthologized [B] among children's poetry, "*The Tiger*" contained [C] fairly complex themes [D].

85. Though often viewed as highly abstruse [A] in his own time, William Blake has became [B] increasingly popular during the twentieth century and was particularly [C] popular with poets and musicians of the 1950s and 1960s [D].

Questions 86-90 are based on the following passage, written by a student.

> Some camels have two humps on their backs, but the dromedary only has one. Dromedaries are popular for carrying things on their backs. They are known to be stubborn and kick people. Dromedaries are very useful to many people in Africa and Saudi Arabia. The dromedary hair is often used by people in these places for tents and clothing. Dromedaries are also eaten. In Egypt, guards use dromedaries instead of horses to keep an eye on the borders.

86. The student is working on primary paragraph elements, including a strong topic sentence. Which of the following would make a good topic sentence for the paragraph that the student has written?

    a. The dromedary is a part of the camel family
    b. Dromedaries are very interesting
    c. The dromedary is not as friendly as the camel
    d. The dromedary is a very useful animal

87. Which of the sentences in the paragraph above does not fit with the primary topic of the paragraph?

    a. Dromedaries are popular for carrying things on their backs
    b. They are known to be stubborn and kick people
    c. Dromedaries are also eaten
    d. In Egypt, guards use dromedaries instead of horses to keep an eye on the borders

88. In order to improve the flow of the paragraph, the instructor recommends that the student incorporate a transitional word or phrase. Which of the following transitional expressions is most appropriate before this sentence: "Dromedaries are very useful to many people in Africa and Saudi Arabia."

    a. As a result
    b. In addition
    c. Although
    d. Perhaps

89. The student is also working on using strong, descriptive language instead of simple words. Which of the following phrase might be a good alternative to the phrase "people in these places"?

　　a. Many who live in Africa and Saudi Arabia
　　b. The people that dwell in these places
　　c. Bedouins living in this part of the world
　　d. The inhabitants here

90. The instructor is concerned about the use of the passive tense in one of the sentences. Which of the following sentences exhibits the use of the passive tense?

　　a. Some camels have two humps on their backs, but the dromedary only has one
　　b. Dromedaries are popular for carrying things on their backs
　　c. Dromedaries are very useful to many people in Africa and Saudi Arabia
　　d. The dromedary hair is often used by people in these places for tents and clothing

Answers and Explanations

Answer Key

1. B	16. C	31. B	46. C	61. A	76. B
2. D	17. A	32. C	47. B	62. B	77. C
3. C	18. D	33. C	48. C	63. B	78. B
4. D	19. B	34. D	49. D	64. B	79. A
5. A	20. D	35. C	50. C	65. D	80. A
6. D	21. A	36. A	51. D	66. A	81. A
7. C	22. B	37. D	52. B	67. C	82. D
8. A	23. D	38. B	53. A	68. A	83. C
9. B	24. C	39. B	54. C	69. D	84. C
10. A	25. A	40. D	55. D	70. D	85. B
11. D	26. B	41. C	56. C	71. B	86. A
12. B	27. D	42. B	57. B	72. B	87. B
13. A	28. C	43. A	58. A	73. B	88. A
14. C	29. C	44. C	59. A	74. A	89. C
15. D	30. B	45. A	60. D	75. C	90. D

1. B: In the first sentence of the passage, the author states, "The benefits of progressive education cannot be ignored in view of the problems caused by the standards-based education system." The author then proceeds to explain the value of progressive education in contrast to the limited scope of standards-based education. Clearly, the main idea of the passage is to indicate the value of progressive education over standards-based education.

2. D: The author contrasts progressive education and standards-based education, arguing that the former is more effective than the latter. The author's clear stance on the issue and use of example to support the primary line of reasoning suggests a purpose of persuasion.

3. C: The author states, "Progressive schools allow for students to learn based on their own strengths, building on knowledge over time. What is more, teachers are encouraged to utilize a variety of procedures and materials to engage students in the learning process." The author then concludes with a statement that standards-based education focuses too much on testing over the "acquisition of real knowledge." These are clear uses of examples to support the main point.

4. D: The author introduces both progressive education and standards-based education and then proceeds to show the differences between the two, weighing one against the other. This indicates the use of a comparison-and-contrast strategy.

5. A: Prior to the sentence noted in the question, the author says, "The progressive education that functioned in the United States through much of the late 19th and 20th centuries provided students with a sound learning foundation." By following this sentence up with a statement about the ongoing value of progressive education in modern schools, the author is using chronology to indicate the continuity of success.

6. D: At the beginning of the passage, the author says, "The benefits of progressive education cannot be ignored in view of the problems caused by the standards-based education system. The possible advantages of the No Child Left Behind reform do little to justify the system that supports it." With

the mention of "problems caused by the standards-based education system" and "possible advantages" viewed as not being enough to justify something negative, it is clear that the author is connecting the No Child Left Behind reform and standards-based education.

7. C: Question 7 is somewhat abstract, so the test-taker should consider each of the various options and eliminate any answer choice that suggests opinion or vague reasoning. This immediately removes answer choices A and D, since expressions like "valuable learning" and "true illumination" cannot be justified in the context of the passage. This leaves only answer choices B and C. At the end of the passage, the author mentions that standards-based education "does not provide the effective acquisition of real knowledge"; this suggests that "real knowledge" is equivalent to Impactful Education.

8. A: The author's tone is scholarly in the sense that the author takes care to provide historical data and examples, and the tone is informative in the sense that the author is clearly intending to inform that reader about the importance of progressive education.

9. B: In the last sentence of the passage, the author says, "Standards-based education, on the other hand, focuses solely on successful testing and does not provide the effective acquisition of real knowledge." Just before this, the author notes that teachers adhering to progressive methods "are encouraged to utilize a variety of procedures and materials to engage students in the learning process." This would suggest that the problems with standards-based education include a focus on testing and a lack of variety.

10. A: Any author employing persuasive strategies has the purpose of encouraging the reader to agree with the stated position, so a preference on the author's part is inevitable.

11. D: Early in the passage, the author says, "In fact, English-only considerations seem to grow in public preferences whenever mainstream English-speaking Americans encounter a non-English-speaking culture in large numbers." This indicates that the English-only movement tends to make an appearance during a time of cultural conflict.

12. B: In the first paragraph, the author focuses on the historical tradition and, thus, the motivation, behind the English-only movement, while in the second paragraph the author brings in the current objections to this movement among educators and linguists.

13. A: With the historical information provided in the first paragraph, the author is utilizing chronology – from the Louisiana Purchase to World War I – to organize the paragraph.

14. C: In combining the two paragraphs, the author uses the chronological details of the first paragraph to represent the cause of the English-only movement, while the information from teachers and linguists represents the potential effect or effects of it.

15. D: At the beginning of the passage, the author says, "With the rise of bilingual education initiatives throughout the United States, the English-only movement has once again become a subject of public debate." At no point in the passage, however, does the author provide a clear source for the recent rise of the English-only movement.

16. C: The author does not take a clear stand on the issue of the English-only movement, but the author's conclusion about the topic suggests a measure of caution. The last sentence in particular offers this tone: "Examples of students penalized for speaking other languages on school buses or with friends in school hallways between classes give reason to worry about the feasibility of any English-only legislation."

17. A: In the first sentence of the second paragraph, the author says, "Despite the English-only push from certain quarters, teachers and language professionals caution that it will cause more harm than good." This indicates an attitude of general concern on the part of teachers and linguists.

18. D: The combination of the information provided in the two paragraphs provides a conclusion that the English-only movement is limited to certain times in history and lends itself to professional concerns (from teachers and linguists) and impractical legislation.

19. B: The author notes in the passage: "He also suggested that instruction is most effective when students do not fear failure and resulting punishment." In other words, effective learning can be hindered by anxiety about the penalties for being wrong.

20. D: At the end of the passage, the author states, "However interesting Skinner's theories were, his claims about human behavior seem to make human beings a little less human." The wording of this statement indicates bias on the author's part.

21. A: At the beginning of the second paragraph, the authors says, "Many historians know, however, that the Phoenicians were not necessarily the first to develop the idea of an alphabet." This would indicate that the author is using a compare-and-contrast method of organization by introducing the idea of the Phoenician alphabet but then explaining that the Phoenicians were not necessary the first to use the alphabet.

22. B: In this case, the best way to assist students in understanding the meaning of the word "script" is to consider the context of the word. In the last sentence, the author states, "Additionally, writing has been found in the areas of Palestine and Sinai, and it indicates another early script that pre-dates the Phoenicians that might have influenced their alphabet." The teacher can remind students that the topic of the passage is alphabets and also point the students' attention to the use of the word "writing" early in this sentence. This should help students in deciphering the meaning of the word "script."

23. D: The main point of the passage is to show that photosynthesis is necessary to provide plants with food and to create a balance in the atmosphere between oxygen and carbon dioxide.

24. C: If the teacher wants students to understand the significance of the balance that photosynthesis helps to maintain, the best question to ask students would be how humans and plants work together. This will require that students consider the symbiotic relationship that occurs during and as a result of photosynthesis.

25. A: By asking the students what would happen if there were not enough plants, the teacher is encouraging the students to think beyond the information and infer consequences based on information in the passage. The teacher can then point out that a shortage of plants results in a potential for a shortage of oxygen and a surplus of carbon dioxide, which leaves the atmosphere imbalanced.

26. B: An affix that is placed at the beginning of a word and alters the inflection of that word is considered a prefix. In this case, "mono" is a prefix that indicates "one" or "alone."

27. D: Reading the sentence carefully, the student should see that the author says, "Akhenaten was so devoted to Aten that he decided to change the religious system within Egypt, and during his reign Egypt became a monotheistic society; in other words, Egyptians began to worship the one god Aten." The only answer choice that can be accurately inferred is that Egyptian society before Akhenaten had involved the worship of many gods.

- 104 -

28. C: An antonym is a word that expresses the opposite of another word. Groupings such as "yes" and "no" represent antonyms, as do groupings such as "remain" and "leave." If the teacher is introducing the concept of antonyms to students, the words "monotheism" and "polytheism" – while not exactly perfect antonyms – can be represented as opposites to elementary students.

29. C: The graph indicates that reading has decreased to a degree, but at the same time the graph suggests that weekly television viewing has increased considerably among elementary children. The graph shows that television watching in 1980 was around ten hours per week, while viewing jumps to around thirty hours per week in 2000.

30. B: Among the answer choices provided, the best option for helping students pronounce new words is to encourage students to sound out the words slowly, keeping the rules of vowels and consonants in mind. This is not, of course, the only option for assisting students with word pronunciation, but it is the best option among the available choices for this question.

31. B: The students making As and Bs represent 70% of the student body. If 53 students make Ds, that is approximately 10% of the student body, leaving the remaining 20% to make Cs.

32. C: Officially, 37% of 461 is 170.57. The rules of rounding require that the number be rounded up, so the approximate answer is 171.

33. C: The test-taker should remember that to divide fractions, the second fraction must be reversed and then multiplied by the other fraction. This means that the test-taker will be multiplying 11/3 (or 3-2/3) by 3/16 (or the reverse of 16/3, which is 5-1/3). The 3s on the top and the bottom cancel each other out, leaving the product 11/16.

34. D: The test-taker must follow the order of operations, which in this case is simply left to right with multiplication and division. (5/6)*(7/3) = (35/18). (35/18)*(5/9) = 175/162.

35. C: Taking 15% off the original price, the computer comes down $105 in value to be $595. Taking 10% off this price (and not the original price of $700), the computer comes down another $59.50. This in addition to the $105 makes for a savings in $164.50.

36. A: When converted to a decimal, 19% is equivalent to .19. The other answer choices place the decimal point in the wrong place and create different percentages than 19%.

37. D: The order of heights, from tallest to shortest, is Anne, Aiden, and Morris. If Anne = x, Aiden = z, and Morris = y, then x > z > y.

38. B: When the number (-3) is filled into the equation $f(x) = x^4 + 2x^3 + 4x -1$, the equation becomes 81-54-12-1, which equals 14.

39. B: To the right of a decimal point, the first number is in the tenths position, and the second number is in the hundredths position. This means that the number 3, which is the second number to the right of the decimal point, is in the hundredths position.

40. D: To determine the total number of students, the test-taker should divide the number that is given (834) by the percentage that is represents (75% or 0.75). The result is 1112 students total in the school. To verify that this is correct, the test-taker may then multiply 1112 by 75% (or 0.75). The result is 834, so the answer is correct.

41. C: The expression (4 + 6)3 is equal to 103 (10 x 10 x 10) or 1000.

42. B: The series is arranged in multiples of 6 in the denominator, with the fraction 1/6 multiplied by 1/2, 1/3, 1/4, 1/5, and so forth. The missing expression is 1/6 x 1/5, which equals 1/30.

43. A: This is a simple multiplication question, with the product of the two expressions being equal to exactly -0.0437.

44. C: The fraction 2/3 may be multiplied by 2/2 to get the denominators equal on both sides of the equation. From here, it is easy to see the 4/6 is less than 5/6.

45. A: When multiplied out, the product equals 16x2 – 12x + 12x – 9. The two middle expressions cancel each other, leaving a product of 16x2 – 9.

46. C: The original number of workers (7) multiplied by the original number of hours to clean Duncombe Park (10) equals 70. By dividing 70 by 14 – the number of hours with the reduced number of workers – the result is a new number of workers: 5.

47. B: With the formula d = rt, the correct answer is largely a matter is filling in the numbers that are provided. Ariadne travels 456 miles (d) in 9 hours (t). By dividing 456 by 9, the rate or speed of her driving may be found. It is important to note that the actual answer is 50.667, which is approximately 50 mi/hr.

48. C: The formula for the area of a triangle is 1/2bh, or one-half the base times the height. This means that the product of the two sides will actually be twice the number that is provided as the area, i.e., 20 x 2 or 40. Although the actual base and height aren't provided, only one answer choice offers two numbers that equal a product of 40 – 8 and 5.

49. D: To locate the mean (or average), it is necessary to add up the numbers that are provided – 15, 23, 8 and 14 – and then divide them by 4. The result is 60 divided by 4, or 15.

50. C: Question 20 is a simple matter of division. The total of 350 grams should be divided by the rate of grams per ounce (or 28) to acquire the number of ounces, in this case 12.5, or just 12.

51. D: The perimeter is found by adding all sides of a figure. In the case of a rectangle, two of the sides are going to be equal in length, so if the width is 10 feet and the height 15 feet, formula would be 10 + 10 + 15 + 15, or 2(10) + 2(15).

52. B: The solution to the correct formula selected in question 21 is 50, because 2(10) + 2(15) is equal to 50.

53. A: Substitute the value (-2/3) for x in each equation and evaluate each one.

For *I*,

$$-3\left(-\frac{2}{3}\right) > -2 + \frac{5}{6\left(-\frac{2}{3}\right)}$$

$$\frac{6}{3} > -2 + \frac{5}{-\frac{12}{3}}$$

$$2 > -2 + \frac{5}{-4}$$

$$2 > -3\frac{1}{4}$$

True

For *II*,

$$3\left(-\frac{2}{3}\right)^2 - 3 \le 12\left(-\frac{2}{3}\right) + 4$$

$$3\left(\frac{4}{9}\right) - 3 \le -\frac{24}{3} + 4$$

$$\frac{12}{9} - 3 \le -8 + 4$$

$$1\frac{1}{3} - 3 \le -4$$

$$-1\frac{2}{3} \le -4$$

False

For *III*,

$$\left|-\frac{2}{3}\right| > 1$$

$$\frac{2}{3} > 1$$

False

Since only inequality *I* is true, the answer is A.

54. C: The equation for finding the slope is (y2 – y1)/(x2 – x1). With the points provided, the equation becomes (5-2)/(3-4), or (3)/(-1): -3.

55. D: The volume formula for a right cylinder is πr2h. The radius of a circle is one-half of its diameter, so with a diameter of 6, the radius of the right cylinder that is described is 3. Using the provided height of 12, the formula becomes π(32)(12), or 108π.

56. C: Reviewing the chart carefully, the only answer choice that may be deduced is that the student Ralph consistently increased his reading from September through December. The chart indicates that Amelia's reading increased during September and October but then decreased in November and December. Likewise Edgar's reading increased during the first two months but showed little improvement during the last two months. (What is more, the chart provides no reason behind the students' improvement or lack thereof, so it is impossible to deduce that Ralph's reading progress was hindered by personal reasons.)

57. B: For the month of December, Amelia's reading is just above 30 pages per week. Of the answer choices provided, answer choice B (or approximately 30) is the best approximation.

58. A: The word problem says that the product of 7 and 6, or (7 x 6) is divided by the sum of 3 and 4, or (3 + 4). This leaves only answer choice A, or (7 x 6)/(3 + 4).

59. A: To find the area of the parallelogram, the area of each shape must be determined and then added together. The area of the smaller triangle is (3 x 5)/2. The area of the rectangle is (3 x 5), and the area of the larger triangle is (4 x 6)/2. This leaves only the formula provided in answer choice A.

60. D: Arriving at the correct answer requires a series of simple steps. The animal skin is said to be 3 feet by 4 feet. In inches, this is 36 inches by 48 inches. This leaves the size to be 36 inches by 48 inches. The area then is 36*48 = 1728. By dividing this by the area of each smaller strip (1*2=2), the answer is 864. 1728/2=864.

61. A: Because of the plural subject documents the very should be refer. "Thirteenth-century legal documents refer…"

62. B: The word legendary is spelled incorrectly in the passage and needs to be changed.

63. B: For correct tense, the verb should be would become: "Maid Marian and Friar Tuck would become..."

64. B: No comma is necessary between story and itself: "...the story itself is just a part..."

65. D: However tempting it is to try to find an error, some sentences on the test can, in fact, be correct. Question 5 is an example, as there is no error in this sentence.

66. A: In this sentence, the word trouvère functions as the object of the preposition, which can be either a noun or a pronoun (i.e., "I gave the book to Jim [noun]," or "I gave the book to him [pronoun]." Because pronoun is not an option, and because it is unlikely that in the context the word trouvère would be a pronoun, the only choice noun.

67. C: The statement "And even the name of the legendary King Arthur" is not a complete sentence and thus cannot stand on its own. The period that is placed before the word And should be removed and the two statements combined.

68. A: The comma that is located before "his Idylls of the King" represents a comma splice and should be replaced with a period, a semicolon, or a comma and a coordinating conjunction. The two statements before and after the comma represent individual sentences and cannot be joined with a comma alone.

69. D: The clue for identifying infinitives is the word to before a verb. In this case, to reflect and to enlighten are excellent examples of infinitives, which are a type of verbal, or a verb form that actually function as a different part of speech. Infinitives (and gerunds) function as nouns.

70. D: The word accommodate needs two c's as well as two m's.

71. B: Because the word but represents a coordinating conjunction that joins two independent clauses, it should have a comma just before it.

72. B: The sentence is in the past tense, so the verb should also be in the past tense: "On the night of his birth, soothsayers prophesied..."

73. B: The phrase "through off" is incorrect (even if it sounds correct). The correct expression should be "threw off."

74. A: To create possession, there should be an apostrophe in the name: "Ivan the Terrible's reforms."

75. C: To modify the verb correctly, the word firm should be converted into the adverb form firmly: "...that would place Russia firmly in the position of a world power."

76. B: The statement in parentheses is an incomplete sentence. In fact, this statement functions as a dependent clause that modifies the word tsar just before it in the sentence. The sentence should read: "...and permanent title of 'tsar' (which his grandfather Ivan III had first used intermittently)."

77. C: No comma is necessary before the conjunction and, which simply joins two items in a series: "...paranoid and unstable."

78. B: The phrase daughter-in-law should be hyphenated so that it represents a single expression, instead of three words.

79. A: The statement beginning "Who is renowned..." is a dependent clause and should be combined with the sentence just before it: "...heirs is Peter the Great who is renowned for..." Note that no comma is necessary before the word who.

80. A: Due to the wording of the sentence, a comma should fall after the date 1917: "The Romanov dynasty ended in 1917, when the last tsar..."

81. A: The wording should be: "Although William Wordsworth is usually remembered as the first major Romantic poet..."

82. D:The use of much is awkward with of his poems and should be revised to read: "...different copies for many of his poems."

83. C: Due to the use of the singular form which the correct verb should be mystifies: "...which still mystifies literary scholars to this day."

84. C: The verb form is inaccurate within the context of the sentence. Because the rest of the sentence indicates a present tense – and because the qualities of the poem remain current – the verb contained should also be adjusted to present tense: "While often anthologized among children's poetry, 'The Tiger' contains fairly complex themes."

85. B: The correct verb form with the word has (or have) is become: "...William Blake has become increasingly popular..."

86. A: Among the options provided, only answer choice A provides a broad enough scope for the information that is provided in the paragraph, ranging from a discussion of dromedaries and camels to the qualities of the dromedary that make it popular. Answer choice B is just an opinion statement and does not necessarily introduce the topic of the paragraph. Answer choice C has little relevance to the information in the paragraph, and answer choice D limits the scope only to the information about the usefulness of the animal. More importantly, though, answer choice D would make no sense when placed at the beginning of the sentence.

87. B: However interesting this information might be, it has no immediate relevance to the details of the paragraph. Had the student explained that dromedaries kick, while camels do not, this information might have gained context. As it is, it is largely superfluous to the topic of the paragraph.

88. A: Question 28 assumes that the test-taker has answer question 27 correctly. With the sentence "They are known to be stubborn and kick people" out of the way, it is easier to see the flow of the paragraph and the value of a transitional expression. In this case, "As a result" best fits the direction that the sentence takes in the paragraph: "Dromedaries are popular for carrying things on their backs. As a result, dromedaries are very useful to many people in Africa and Saudi Arabia."

89. C: The word Bedouin is very specific and also provides some idea of the people group for whom dromedary hair is useful. The other answer choices, while slightly better than the statement in the sentence (with the possible exception of answer choice D) are not as strong and descriptive as answer choice C.

90. D: A sentence in the passive tense reverses the subject and object roles, so that the subject of the sentence becomes the object or recipient of the action: "The book was given to Harold by Hanna," instead of "Hanna gave the book to Harold." Writing instructors strongly recommend avoiding the passive tense and utilizing the active tense instead. In the paragraph provided, the sentence would

more comfortably read: "People in these places [or Bedouins living in this part of the world] often use the dromedary hair for tents and clothing."

How to Overcome Test Anxiety

Just the thought of taking a test is enough to make most people a little nervous. A test is an important event that can have a long-term impact on your future, so it's important to take it seriously and it's natural to feel anxious about performing well. But just because anxiety is normal, that doesn't mean that it's helpful in test taking, or that you should simply accept it as part of your life. Anxiety can have a variety of effects. These effects can be mild, like making you feel slightly nervous, or severe, like blocking your ability to focus or remember even a simple detail.

If you experience test anxiety—whether severe or mild—it's important to know how to beat it. To discover this, first you need to understand what causes test anxiety.

Causes of Test Anxiety

While we often think of anxiety as an uncontrollable emotional state, it can actually be caused by simple, practical things. One of the most common causes of test anxiety is that a person does not feel adequately prepared for their test. This feeling can be the result of many different issues such as poor study habits or lack of organization, but the most common culprit is time management. Starting to study too late, failing to organize your study time to cover all of the material, or being distracted while you study will mean that you're not well prepared for the test. This may lead to cramming the night before, which will cause you to be physically and mentally exhausted for the test. Poor time management also contributes to feelings of stress, fear, and hopelessness as you realize you are not well prepared but don't know what to do about it.

Other times, test anxiety is not related to your preparation for the test but comes from unresolved fear. This may be a past failure on a test, or poor performance on tests in general. It may come from comparing yourself to others who seem to be performing better or from the stress of living up to expectations. Anxiety may be driven by fears of the future—how failure on this test would affect your educational and career goals. These fears are often completely irrational, but they can still negatively impact your test performance.

> **Review Video:** 3 Reasons You Have Test Anxiety
> Visit mometrix.com/academy and enter code: 428468

Elements of Test Anxiety

As mentioned earlier, test anxiety is considered to be an emotional state, but it has physical and mental components as well. Sometimes you may not even realize that you are suffering from test anxiety until you notice the physical symptoms. These can include trembling hands, rapid heartbeat, sweating, nausea, and tense muscles. Extreme anxiety may lead to fainting or vomiting. Obviously, any of these symptoms can have a negative impact on testing. It is important to recognize them as soon as they begin to occur so that you can address the problem before it damages your performance.

> **Review Video: 3 Ways to Tell You Have Test Anxiety**
> Visit mometrix.com/academy and enter code: 927847

The mental components of test anxiety include trouble focusing and inability to remember learned information. During a test, your mind is on high alert, which can help you recall information and stay focused for an extended period of time. However, anxiety interferes with your mind's natural processes, causing you to blank out, even on the questions you know well. The strain of testing during anxiety makes it difficult to stay focused, especially on a test that may take several hours. Extreme anxiety can take a huge mental toll, making it difficult not only to recall test information but even to understand the test questions or pull your thoughts together.

> **Review Video: How Test Anxiety Affects Memory**
> Visit mometrix.com/academy and enter code: 609003

Effects of Test Anxiety

Test anxiety is like a disease—if left untreated, it will get progressively worse. Anxiety leads to poor performance, and this reinforces the feelings of fear and failure, which in turn lead to poor performances on subsequent tests. It can grow from a mild nervousness to a crippling condition. If allowed to progress, test anxiety can have a big impact on your schooling, and consequently on your future.

Test anxiety can spread to other parts of your life. Anxiety on tests can become anxiety in any stressful situation, and blanking on a test can turn into panicking in a job situation. But fortunately, you don't have to let anxiety rule your testing and determine your grades. There are a number of relatively simple steps you can take to move past anxiety and function normally on a test and in the rest of life.

> **Review Video: How Test Anxiety Impacts Your Grades**
> Visit mometrix.com/academy and enter code: 939819

Physical Steps for Beating Test Anxiety

While test anxiety is a serious problem, the good news is that it can be overcome. It doesn't have to control your ability to think and remember information. While it may take time, you can begin taking steps today to beat anxiety.

Just as your first hint that you may be struggling with anxiety comes from the physical symptoms, the first step to treating it is also physical. Rest is crucial for having a clear, strong mind. If you are tired, it is much easier to give in to anxiety. But if you establish good sleep habits, your body and mind will be ready to perform optimally, without the strain of exhaustion. Additionally, sleeping well helps you to retain information better, so you're more likely to recall the answers when you see the test questions.

Getting good sleep means more than going to bed on time. It's important to allow your brain time to relax. Take study breaks from time to time so it doesn't get overworked, and don't study right before bed. Take time to rest your mind before trying to rest your body, or you may find it difficult to fall asleep.

> **Review Video: The Importance of Sleep for Your Brain**
> Visit mometrix.com/academy and enter code: 319338

Along with sleep, other aspects of physical health are important in preparing for a test. Good nutrition is vital for good brain function. Sugary foods and drinks may give a burst of energy but this burst is followed by a crash, both physically and emotionally. Instead, fuel your body with protein and vitamin-rich foods.

Also, drink plenty of water. Dehydration can lead to headaches and exhaustion, especially if your brain is already under stress from the rigors of the test. Particularly if your test is a long one, drink water during the breaks. And if possible, take an energy-boosting snack to eat between sections.

> **Review Video: How Diet Can Affect your Mood**
> Visit mometrix.com/academy and enter code: 624317

Along with sleep and diet, a third important part of physical health is exercise. Maintaining a steady workout schedule is helpful, but even taking 5-minute study breaks to walk can help get your blood pumping faster and clear your head. Exercise also releases endorphins, which contribute to a positive feeling and can help combat test anxiety.

When you nurture your physical health, you are also contributing to your mental health. If your body is healthy, your mind is much more likely to be healthy as well. So take time to rest, nourish your body with healthy food and water, and get moving as much as possible. Taking these physical steps will make you stronger and more able to take the mental steps necessary to overcome test anxiety.

> **Review Video: How to Stay Healthy and Prevent Test Anxiety**
> Visit mometrix.com/academy and enter code: 877894

Mental Steps for Beating Test Anxiety

Working on the mental side of test anxiety can be more challenging, but as with the physical side, there are clear steps you can take to overcome it. As mentioned earlier, test anxiety often stems from lack of preparation, so the obvious solution is to prepare for the test. Effective studying may be the most important weapon you have for beating test anxiety, but you can and should employ several other mental tools to combat fear.

First, boost your confidence by reminding yourself of past success—tests or projects that you aced. If you're putting as much effort into preparing for this test as you did for those, there's no reason you should expect to fail here. Work hard to prepare; then trust your preparation.

Second, surround yourself with encouraging people. It can be helpful to find a study group, but be sure that the people you're around will encourage a positive attitude. If you spend time with others who are anxious or cynical, this will only contribute to your own anxiety. Look for others who are motivated to study hard from a desire to succeed, not from a fear of failure.

Third, reward yourself. A test is physically and mentally tiring, even without anxiety, and it can be helpful to have something to look forward to. Plan an activity following the test, regardless of the outcome, such as going to a movie or getting ice cream.

When you are taking the test, if you find yourself beginning to feel anxious, remind yourself that you know the material. Visualize successfully completing the test. Then take a few deep, relaxing breaths and return to it. Work through the questions carefully but with confidence, knowing that you are capable of succeeding.

Developing a healthy mental approach to test taking will also aid in other areas of life. Test anxiety affects more than just the actual test—it can be damaging to your mental health and even contribute to depression. It's important to beat test anxiety before it becomes a problem for more than testing.

Review Video: Test Anxiety and Depression
Visit mometrix.com/academy and enter code: 904704

Study Strategy

Being prepared for the test is necessary to combat anxiety, but what does being prepared look like? You may study for hours on end and still not feel prepared. What you need is a strategy for test prep. The next few pages outline our recommended steps to help you plan out and conquer the challenge of preparation.

Step 1: Scope Out the Test

Learn everything you can about the format (multiple choice, essay, etc.) and what will be on the test. Gather any study materials, course outlines, or sample exams that may be available. Not only will this help you to prepare, but knowing what to expect can help to alleviate test anxiety.

Step 2: Map Out the Material

Look through the textbook or study guide and make note of how many chapters or sections it has. Then divide these over the time you have. For example, if a book has 15 chapters and you have five days to study, you need to cover three chapters each day. Even better, if you have the time, leave an extra day at the end for overall review after you have gone through the material in depth.

If time is limited, you may need to prioritize the material. Look through it and make note of which sections you think you already have a good grasp on, and which need review. While you are studying, skim quickly through the familiar sections and take more time on the challenging parts. Write out your plan so you don't get lost as you go. Having a written plan also helps you feel more in control of the study, so anxiety is less likely to arise from feeling overwhelmed at the amount to cover. A sample plan may look like this:

- Day 1: Skim chapters 1–4, study chapter 5 (especially pages 31–33)
- Day 2: Study chapters 6–7, skim chapters 8–9
- Day 3: Skim chapter 10, study chapters 11–12 (especially pages 87–90)
- Day 4: Study chapters 13–15
- Day 5: Overall review (focus most on chapters 5, 6, and 12), take practice test

Step 3: Gather Your Tools

Decide what study method works best for you. Do you prefer to highlight in the book as you study and then go back over the highlighted portions? Or do you type out notes of the important information? Or is it helpful to make flashcards that you can carry with you? Assemble the pens, index cards, highlighters, post-it notes, and any other materials you may need so you won't be distracted by getting up to find things while you study.

If you're having a hard time retaining the information or organizing your notes, experiment with different methods. For example, try color-coding by subject with colored pens, highlighters, or post-it notes. If you learn better by hearing, try recording yourself reading your notes so you can listen while in the car, working out, or simply sitting at your desk. Ask a friend to quiz you from your flashcards, or try teaching someone the material to solidify it in your mind.

Step 4: Create Your Environment

It's important to avoid distractions while you study. This includes both the obvious distractions like visitors and the subtle distractions like an uncomfortable chair (or a too-comfortable couch that makes you want to fall asleep). Set up the best study environment possible: good lighting and a comfortable work area. If background music helps you focus, you may want to turn it on, but otherwise keep the room quiet. If you are using a computer to take notes, be sure you don't have any other windows open, especially applications like social media, games, or anything else that could distract you. Silence your phone and turn off notifications. Be sure to keep water close by so you stay hydrated while you study (but avoid unhealthy drinks and snacks).

Also, take into account the best time of day to study. Are you freshest first thing in the morning? Try to set aside some time then to work through the material. Is your mind clearer in the afternoon or evening? Schedule your study session then. Another method is to study at the same time of day that you will take the test, so that your brain gets used to working on the material at that time and will be ready to focus at test time.

Step 5: Study!

Once you have done all the study preparation, it's time to settle into the actual studying. Sit down, take a few moments to settle your mind so you can focus, and begin to follow your study plan. Don't give in to distractions or let yourself procrastinate. This is your time to prepare so you'll be ready to fearlessly approach the test. Make the most of the time and stay focused.

Of course, you don't want to burn out. If you study too long you may find that you're not retaining the information very well. Take regular study breaks. For example, taking five minutes out of every hour to walk briskly, breathing deeply and swinging your arms, can help your mind stay fresh.

As you get to the end of each chapter or section, it's a good idea to do a quick review. Remind yourself of what you learned and work on any difficult parts. When you feel that you've mastered the material, move on to the next part. At the end of your study session, briefly skim through your notes again.

But while review is helpful, cramming last minute is NOT. If at all possible, work ahead so that you won't need to fit all your study into the last day. Cramming overloads your brain with more information than it can process and retain, and your tired mind may struggle to recall even previously learned information when it is overwhelmed with last-minute study. Also, the urgent nature of cramming and the stress placed on your brain contribute to anxiety. You'll be more likely to go to the test feeling unprepared and having trouble thinking clearly.

So don't cram, and don't stay up late before the test, even just to review your notes at a leisurely pace. Your brain needs rest more than it needs to go over the information again. In fact, plan to finish your studies by noon or early afternoon the day before the test. Give your brain the rest of the day to relax or focus on other things, and get a good night's sleep. Then you will be fresh for the test and better able to recall what you've studied.

Step 6: Take a practice test

Many courses offer sample tests, either online or in the study materials. This is an excellent resource to check whether you have mastered the material, as well as to prepare for the test format and environment.

Check the test format ahead of time: the number of questions, the type (multiple choice, free response, etc.), and the time limit. Then create a plan for working through them. For example, if you have 30 minutes to take a 60-question test, your limit is 30 seconds per question. Spend less time on the questions you know well so that you can take more time on the difficult ones.

If you have time to take several practice tests, take the first one open book, with no time limit. Work through the questions at your own pace and make sure you fully understand them. Gradually work up to taking a test under test conditions: sit at a desk with all study materials put away and set a timer. Pace yourself to make sure you finish the test with time to spare and go back to check your answers if you have time.

After each test, check your answers. On the questions you missed, be sure you understand why you missed them. Did you misread the question (tests can use tricky wording)? Did you forget the information? Or was it something you hadn't learned? Go back and study any shaky areas that the practice tests reveal.

Taking these tests not only helps with your grade, but also aids in combating test anxiety. If you're already used to the test conditions, you're less likely to worry about it, and working through tests until you're scoring well gives you a confidence boost. Go through the practice tests until you feel comfortable, and then you can go into the test knowing that you're ready for it.

Test Tips

On test day, you should be confident, knowing that you've prepared well and are ready to answer the questions. But aside from preparation, there are several test day strategies you can employ to maximize your performance.

First, as stated before, get a good night's sleep the night before the test (and for several nights before that, if possible). Go into the test with a fresh, alert mind rather than staying up late to study.

Try not to change too much about your normal routine on the day of the test. It's important to eat a nutritious breakfast, but if you normally don't eat breakfast at all, consider eating just a protein bar. If you're a coffee drinker, go ahead and have your normal coffee. Just make sure you time it so that the caffeine doesn't wear off right in the middle of your test. Avoid sugary beverages, and drink enough water to stay hydrated but not so much that you need a restroom break 10 minutes into the test. If your test isn't first thing in the morning, consider going for a walk or doing a light workout before the test to get your blood flowing.

Allow yourself enough time to get ready, and leave for the test with plenty of time to spare so you won't have the anxiety of scrambling to arrive in time. Another reason to be early is to select a good seat. It's helpful to sit away from doors and windows, which can be distracting. Find a good seat, get out your supplies, and settle your mind before the test begins.

When the test begins, start by going over the instructions carefully, even if you already know what to expect. Make sure you avoid any careless mistakes by following the directions.

Then begin working through the questions, pacing yourself as you've practiced. If you're not sure on an answer, don't spend too much time on it, and don't let it shake your confidence. Either skip it and come back later, or eliminate as many wrong answers as possible and guess among the remaining ones. Don't dwell on these questions as you continue—put them out of your mind and focus on what lies ahead.

Be sure to read all of the answer choices, even if you're sure the first one is the right answer. Sometimes you'll find a better one if you keep reading. But don't second-guess yourself if you do immediately know the answer. Your gut instinct is usually right. Don't let test anxiety rob you of the information you know.

If you have time at the end of the test (and if the test format allows), go back and review your answers. Be cautious about changing any, since your first instinct tends to be correct, but make sure you didn't misread any of the questions or accidentally mark the wrong answer choice. Look over any you skipped and make an educated guess.

At the end, leave the test feeling confident. You've done your best, so don't waste time worrying about your performance or wishing you could change anything. Instead, celebrate the successful completion of this test. And finally, use this test to learn how to deal with anxiety even better next time.

> **Review Video: 5 Tips to Beat Test Anxiety**
> Visit mometrix.com/academy and enter code: 570656

Important Qualification

Not all anxiety is created equal. If your test anxiety is causing major issues in your life beyond the classroom or testing center, or if you are experiencing troubling physical symptoms related to your anxiety, it may be a sign of a serious physiological or psychological condition. If this sounds like your situation, we strongly encourage you to seek professional help.

Thank You

We at Mometrix would like to extend our heartfelt thanks to you, our friend and patron, for allowing us to play a part in your journey. It is a privilege to serve people from all walks of life who are unified in their commitment to building the best future they can for themselves.

The preparation you devote to these important testing milestones may be the most valuable educational opportunity you have for making a real difference in your life. We encourage you to put your heart into it—that feeling of succeeding, overcoming, and yes, conquering will be well worth the hours you've invested.

We want to hear your story, your struggles and your successes, and if you see any opportunities for us to improve our materials so we can help others even more effectively in the future, please share that with us as well. **The team at Mometrix would be absolutely thrilled to hear from you!** So please, send us an email (support@mometrix.com) and let's stay in touch.

If you'd like some additional help, check out these other resources we offer for your exam:

http://MometrixFlashcards.com/GACE

Additional Bonus Material

Due to our efforts to try to keep this book to a manageable length, we've created a link that will give you access to all of your additional bonus material.

Please visit http://www.mometrix.com/bonus948/gaceparapro to access the information.